Faith
Bill Skeeha

VATICAN II - A PROMISE BROKEN?

JOSEPH D. DILLON

EDWARD G. JEEP

In this small book we have used ideas from many people and have noted the sources. The reference information has been inserted informally into the text. Cover design by Elizabeth Jeep, 2010.

First published by the Skeehan Project June 2010

ISBN: 1453651535
EAN-13: 9781453651537

Copies available from
Joe Dillon at dillcj@sbcglobal.net
or Jerry Jeep at egjeep@sbcglobal.net

DEDICATION

The authors extend their gratitude to Rev. William Skeehan for graciously allowing them to write this theological reflection on his experience as pastor of two Catholic parishes during the years following the Second Vatican Council. The leadership, trust and deep regard that Bill offered to the parishioners and neighbors with whom he worked was reciprocated, resulting in two remarkable communities that fully embodied the prophetic vision, pastoral creativity and "true Christian spirit" that the Council had promised.

JOE DILLON AND JERRY JEEP

JUNE 2010

TABLE OF CONTENTS

WHAT A VATICAN II PARISH LOOKS LIKE

by Joseph D. Dillon

What Vatican II Stood For

This is the story of two Oklahoma parishes that were created in the spirit of the Second Vatican Council, Resurrection Parish in Tulsa, Oklahoma and The Community of St. James in Bartlesville, Oklahoma.

In 1968, some three years after the close of the Council, Bishop Victor J. Reed of the Oklahoma City-Tulsa diocese, invited Father Bill Skeehan to start an experimental parish in South Tulsa, a middle class and upper-middle class socio-economic area.

The story of the two parishes is also the story of the pastor, the aforementioned Bill Skeehan, whom the bishop recognized as one filled with the spirit that had flowed from the Council as well as the skill to put that spirit into a parish structure.

Since these two parishes and their pastor represented the renewal that came forth from the Council, it is important that we capture briefly what this revolutionary event, spread over four sessions from 1962 to 1965, was all about.

What kind of pope convened Vatican II? Angelo Roncalli was a grandfatherly man of 79 when he was elected pope. It was facetiously said at the time that at his age he would not be able "to rock the boat" by being pope for a long time. The much-loved Pope John 23 was a man unashamed of his peasant origin, a humble man blessed with a sense of humor and the common touch, a wise man of broad vision, owing to his sense of history and his experience as nuncio to such diverse countries as Bulgaria, Turkey, and France. Above all, he was a prayerful man.

In John's opening remarks to the Council, he mentioned four specific purposes:

- to <u>renew</u> the Catholic Church so that it might more faithfully reflect the gospel of Jesus;

- to <u>reunite</u> the divided Church of Christ;

- to <u>apply</u> the gospel of Christ to the great problems of the world so that the human family might live in peace and justice; and

- to <u>modernize</u> or update the church.

Thus did Pope John 23 challenge the 2,540 assembled bishops to bring a new spirit and direction to the Catholic Church.

As the bishops began to work, a split soon developed between the traditional bishops resistant to change, who understood the church according to the Council of Trent and Counter-Reformation theology and practices, and progressive bishops, who valued aggiornamento according to the signs of the times, and wanted the church to change in its worship, its disciplinary practice, and even in its doctrinal formulations. This struggle between the two opposing views was brought into the open in the very first session when a traditional understanding of the Church of the last 400 years was rejected by a majority of the bishops. Bishop DeSmedt from Bruges, Belgium, criticized the first draft of a document on the church as being triumphalistic (a superiority attitude), clericalistic (bishops and priests dominating the laity) and legalistic (too law-centered), thus failing to emphasize the larger "law of Love" that is the gospel of Jesus.

The two theologies of church have been popularly visualized as a pyramid with pope, bishops, priests on top and the non-ordained lay Christians below (traditional Roman ecclesiology) or as a large circle made up of all the baptized with the hierarchy in the center serving rather than dominating the people (newer ecclesiology).

This circular structure of the church emphasizing equality of persons with different functions became embedded in Bill Skeehan's understanding and in his ministry.

We now turn to Avery Dulles, an American ecclesiologist who outlined ten basic principles endorsed by the Council:

1. Aggiornamento – The Church with its magnificent heritage should not allow itself to become a museum piece.

2. The Reformability of the Church – Vatican II called the church the people of God, a pilgrim people, capable of sin and in need of continual reformation.

3. Renewed Attention to the Word of God - With the counter-Reformation emphasis on law and sacraments, Catholics too often neglected the spiritual riches of the Bible.

4. Collegiality – The sharing of decision-making and collaboration at all levels of the church, from pope and bishops to priests and laity, is one of the most important aspects of the renewal of the church envisioned by the Council.

5. Religious Freedom – This revolutionary declaration is summarized as follows, "the right to freedom in religions and freedom to seek the truth, embrace it, adhere to it, and act on it inheres in each man and woman by reason of his/her dignity as a person endowed with reason and free will and, therefore, endowed with conscience and personal responsibility." This revolution in Catholic thought was largely the

contribution of the American Jesuit, John Courtney Murray, recognizing for the first time in Catholic thought the theological principle of the <u>development of doctrine</u> as expressed by Cardinal Newman.

6. <u>Active Role of the Laity</u> – <u>The Decree on the Apostolate of the Laity</u> exhorted laypersons "to exercise their apostolate in the Church and in the world, both in the spiritual and temporal orders."

7. <u>Regional and Local Variety</u> – This emphasis on the local churches, each under the direction of a bishop was designed to offset the centralization of power and decision-making in Rome which had been increasing ever since Trent.

8. <u>Ecumenism</u> – Accepting the validity of other Christian churches and working for the full unity of Christ's one Church was to become a characteristic of Catholics.

9. <u>Dialogue with Other Religions</u> – Though Vatican II continued to insist on the God-given uniqueness of the Church of Christ, nonetheless, it moved the church into respectful dialogue with the great world religions, especially Judaism.

10. <u>The Social Mission of the Church</u> – This commitment of the church working for the kingdom of God on earth precisely as part of its

gospel mission is the result of John 23's open-
ness to the world in which the church began to
assume responsibility to teach the principles of a
just social order.

Editorial note: This brief review of what the Second Vatican
Council stood for is paraphrased from a book by Joseph F. Eagan,
Restoration and Renewal: The Church in the Third Millennium
(Kansas City: Sheed and Ward, 1995) 21-24. Eagan's quotes from
Avery Dulles are taken from *The Reshaping of Catholicism:
Current Challenges in the Theology of Church* (San Francisco:
Harper and Row, 1988) 19-33. In all cases the emphases are
added.

Background

What were some of the influences that shaped the
person who as a relatively young priest would be
selected by Bishop Reed to establish an experimental
parish? Unfortunately, we don't have a lot of background information on Bill Skeehan, but we will share
what we have learned.

Bill was born in New York on December 8, 1926, three
years prior to the Great Depression of the 1930s. He
was the youngest of five children, and as so often
happens with families of that size, the three older
children, Bud, Mary and Jack (sister and two brothers)
formed a sibling group, and the two younger children,
Bill and his sister Pat, who was a year older, formed
another sibling group. The family experienced a
tragedy when Bud, the eldest child, was killed serving

his country during World War II. The three older children are now deceased.

Bill's father, Edward Michael, became the Chief Financial Officer for the Barnsdall Oil Co. It seems that he started with Barnsdall in New York City and was involved in several transfers between Tulsa, Oklahoma, and Los Angeles, California. When Bill was 13, his father was again transferred to Tulsa, which at that time was known as "the oil capitol of the world."

Mr. Skeehan was through and through a business man, somewhat of a genius with numbers. Bill doesn't recall ever seeing his dad without a tie on and reflects that he wasn't keen on taking part in social events. As with many men of that era, he was reluctant to give hugs and rarely let his emotions show.

It was obvious that Bill had a loving regard for his mother, Eva. For example, when Bishop McGuinness offered Bill the opportunity to study theology at the renowned Louvain University in Belgium, he didn't accept because his mother was in poor health at the time and he chose not to be separated from her for four years.

In a recent conversation, as Bill and Pat looked back on their lives, Pat became aware that she was often selected as the head, the leader of this or that. Bill then realized that he also was a natural born leader. He was president of his grade school class, president of his fraternity, and later, national president of fraternities. Even as a newly ordained priest, he was appointed as the head of the younger priests on the diocesan council. This would prove to be a valuable trait as he took on the responsibility of a parish.

Bill was a popular student at Marquette High School in Tulsa, from 1940 to1944. He had left behind his affinity for the ocean and prowess as a body surfer for an active social life and stellar career as a football offensive guard and defensive linebacker.

He received his B.A. degree in commercial art from the University of Tulsa in 1948. He worked as a freelance artist in Los Angeles and Tulsa before entering St. Thomas Seminary in Denver. He graduated and was ordained in 1960.

There is an interesting story about what led to his going to the Seminary. He suffered a traumatic encounter with a cousin-in-law at a Notre Dame Club party in May of 1954. In a conversation with Katie Deck Skeehan (married to Bill's cousin, Bob Skeehan), she suddenly said, "Bill, you are the most self-centered person I know!" Bill was stunned. He respected her and he went over and over the remark that night. Lo and behold, he swallowed his pride, decided she was right, and called her the next day to thank her.

This was the moment of conversion in his life. For Paul of Tarsus, it took place on the way to Damascus; for

Bill of Tulsa, it took place at a social event. He started talking to priests he admired, among whom were Bill Nerin, Maurice Statham, Monsignor Rooney, and especially his mentor, Jim McNamee.

Soon after the seed had been planted, Bill and his good friend, Jerry Jeep, got out of their car in front of a pub at 8th and Main streets in downtown Tulsa, and over the top of the car simultaneously announced to one another "I've decided to go to the Seminary."

Off to the Seminary

Like any number of men with "delayed vocations" studying for the priesthood, Bill Skeehan found his six years at St. Thomas Seminary in Denver a disappointing experience. Seminaries at the time were often caricatured as "a place where men were turned into boys." St. Thomas was simply not a quality graduate academic institution with a well-prepared faculty. The professors, for the most part, did not welcome questions or open their classrooms to vibrant discussions, and for whatever reason, the administration did not tolerate discussion groups by the students themselves outside of class.

The one memorable exception was the scripture classes taught by Bruce Vawter, CM. Vawter's classes were characterized as an excellent learning situation in which students were exposed to the state-of-the-art in contemporary biblical studies.

Despite the drawbacks of the seminary system, the students, on their own, kept up with the exciting developments happening at Vatican II across the Atlantic in Rome, Italy, by smuggling in the outstanding books of the prominent theologians of the time.

Sacred Heart, Oklahoma City 1960-1965

Fortunately, Bishop Reed gave Bill a plum first assignment. He became an assistant to Msgr. Sylvester Luecke at Sacred Heart Parish in S.E. Oklahoma City. As vicar general of the diocese, Luecke was Bishop Reed's right hand man in charge of several significant projects. The Luecke family from the farming community of Okeene, was well-known in Catholic circles in Oklahoma, because Luecke also had three sisters who had become Benedictine nuns and served as outstanding teachers in various schools throughout the state. They were Marie (Gregory), Liguori (Leona) and Jane Marie.

Luecke was a down-to-earth guy, who was much admired by his fellow priests and the lay people of the diocese. He served as a valuable mentor to Bill as he was learning the ropes of being a priest.

Dan Allen was already an assistant at Sacred Heart when Bill arrived. Dan had also attended Marquette High School in Tulsa, and graduated in 1949, five years after Bill had graduated. Bill and Dan were not only assigned to Sacred Heart Parish, but also taught religion at Mount St. Mary's High School, run by the Sisters of Mercy.

The changes stemming from the Council were bringing about an exciting ferment at the Diocese of Oklahoma City and Tulsa, and part of the excitement came from the arrival of a group of young women who were graduates of Catholic colleges throughout the U.S. Originally these women, willing to dedicate one year to the service of the church, were known as Oklahoma Volunteers. Later, as the program was taken over by the missionary organization, The Extension Society, they became known as Extension Volunteers.

Bill and Dan played a key role in the development of the program and were responsible, to a large extent, for the spiritual training of the volunteers. One of their contributions, in which Dan had the lead role, was the production of a magnificent Training Manual based on the Gospel of Matthew's notion of the Kingdom of God, and how the volunteers were part of that Kingdom in Oklahoma.

Working together with Dan, rubbing elbows, and learning from one another, led to a life-long friendship. Bill often referred to their relationship as "the odd couple", because they came from vastly different backgrounds. Bill had been raised in affluence in both Los Angeles and Tulsa, whereas Dan grew up in a large family that lived in St. Francis Parish in Tulsa. It was an area where Dan learned the ins and outs of poverty during the depression era of the '30s.

A few years later, when both had assignments in the Tulsa area, they collaborated in a remarkable poverty program, Neighbor for Neighbor. Dan founded NfN and Bill served as chairman of the Board of Directors for several years.

Bill expressed his profound gratitude for what Dan had meant to him when he delivered the following homily on the occasion of Dan's Mass of Resurrection at Holy Family Cathedral in downtown Tulsa.

MASS OF THE RESURRECTION
Daniel Richard Allen
Died November of 1955

AMOS 5:7-13, 21-24; JAMES 5:1-6; MATTHEW 25:31-40

Homily by Fr. Bill Skeehan

If I believed in reincarnation, I would have to suspect that James (the author of the Epistle) has come back as Dan Allen, and perhaps Amos had come back as James. Appropriately, James was the least popular of the major New Testament writers. Small wonder. For James, like Dan (and of course, like Jesus), based his teaching of justice upon the fundamental distinction between the rich and the poor. God's love comes close to the poor and lowly, the least of the brothers and sisters. The rich must find a way of standing at their side if they, too, are to know God's acceptance. In Christ, according to James and Dan, all are equal; nevertheless, if God could be said to have favorites, it would be the poor who would be singled out for God's predilection. To draw close to the poor by coming to their aid is equivalent, in James' and Dan's view, to drawing close to God. In his own words (24 years ago) from the original mission statement of Neighbor for Neighbor, Dan put it this way: "We are changing the attitude of the affluent. Their contact with the poor makes them aware that they, the affluent, have created the poor, therefore, they can recreate, both in the society of the poor and in their own environment."

As one of Dan's nephews put it, "Dan was above all a teacher." He was above all a teacher because he was below it all; streetwise, incarnate among the poor; he was there, present! (He understood; that is, stood under, not over.)

Dan did not practice what he preached – he preached what he practiced. He was what he practiced; it came from his very being, and that's why he appeared so authentic, so real, because he was. (It was a graced gift he was open to.)

James and Dan call us to look carefully at our own interior attitudes and to ask just how they are reflected in what we do. They insist that our faith has to be enfleshed if it is to have credibility. Dan looks at corporate America and says with James: "Behold the worker's wage...kept back from them by you...calls out against you!" Matthew's parable speaks of the least of Christ's brothers and sisters. Down at the farm where Dan, Pickett and I spent twenty years of Mondays, Dan's concern for the least was vividly seen. When he mowed the acreage, he was extremely careful not to mow down any weed that was blooming. The rich variety of blooming weeds fascinated him far more the normal ordinary flowers that we care for. This innate sensibility was obviously reflected in Dan's association with the least of the poor–those who simply ceased to exist, for example, as economic persons, invisible to all lending institutions.

The last thing Dan said to me, the night before surgery as I was leaving–he turned in the doorway and said, "Bill, pray for me." Dan was a believer with substance. As reported by Father Monahan in the magazine Salt of the Earth, *Dan understood Eucharist to be for the sake of those present, so they will become God's love for the many. When we say in the Eucharistic Prayer, "This is my body..., my blood... for you and for the many," all too often we forget about the many. For Dan they were the many of "I was hungry, I was naked."*

It could be said that Dan used colorful language. Well, yes, but he swore about something decent. He swore out of justified anger, because the "least" were getting less. We swear because we, who already have too much, want more.

Monahan again says it well: "Dan Allen's bearded face is a mosaic of the sadness of poverty provoked by damaging greed, and an articulate sense of humor which bubbles up from a deep well of hope in the reign of God."

There was a splendid editorial in The Tulsa World *this morning on Dan. Let me share with you the last two paragraphs:*

> *"To those who didn't know him, the gruff and plain-spoken Allen may have seemed an unlikely candidate to be the chief advocate for the poor people. But to those who knew him well, those traits and others made him the lovable and unforgettable character that he was.*

> *The people who Allen brought on board and trained in poverty-fighting techniques no doubt will try hard to carry out the vision that the once-dubbed 'radical priest' strived for his entire adult life. They will succeed, because his dedication, enthusiasm and timelessness were infectious. But they will never replace him. Dan Allen was one of a kind."*

Jesus said that whoever cared for the "least" would enter eternal life. This morning Jesus is saying, "Welcome, Dan, into the Kingdom, for wherever I am there you will be."

To Dance with a Cross on our Back: Reflections on the Word Made Flesh (Bartlesville OK: Meddlers Books, 1998)22-25.

End of Homily

As a further tribute to the memory of Dan Allen, we are including The Mission Statement of Neighbor for Neighbor.

Neighbor for Neighbor: Mission of the Free Clinic

The folks...at Neighbor for Neighbor meet the Word-made-flesh when they sit across the desk from the volunteer during intake. 'In-take' – one of those funny clinical words we use – is 'taking in' that person, at that moment, with unconditional personal regard for the whole person sitting there: flesh and blood and spirit...the interview creating a kinder, gentler environment for the sick. This is a holy moment. People meet the Word-made-flesh through the nurse's loving touch, the nurse who makes no judgment about the patient's clothes or smell or lice in the scalp. That is a holy moment. People meet the Word-made-flesh through the doctor whose skilled hands, intelligent mind and gentle heart listen well and respond with compassion. This is a holy moment. People meet the

Word-made-flesh through the medical technicians who patiently and carefully test the body fluids. This is a holy moment.

Neighbor for Neighbor Was a holy moment!
<u>Not</u> a corporation

In 1964, at the relatively young age of 50, Msgr. Luecke, the tireless worker, suddenly died of a heart attack. Dan Allen had been assigned as pastor to a rural parish in Marshall, OK, so it was left to Bill to be named interim pastor at Sacred Heart for a short time.

While still at Sacred Heart, Bill made a comment that his priest colleagues frequently reminded him of, "When I enter the pulpit, I always have my Bible Missal in one hand and the daily newspaper in the other hand." It was a telling comment, for already it meant, as a young priest, he was learning to take the words and actions of Jesus of Nazareth and applying them to the events of the day. He was learning to read "the signs of the times" and speak of them in a prophetic sense that would be so characteristic of his later homilies.

St. Joseph's, Norman, 1965-1968

From interim pastor at Sacred Heart, Bill was assigned as assistant to St. Joseph's Parish in the Oklahoma University college town of Norman. Father Jim Traut was Pastor. Bill described Traut as a good man who regrettably was suffering from alcoholism. The pastoral situation was such that Jim Traut gave Bill free rein to pretty much do whatever he wanted.

This was a heady time in the Church, especially in Oklahoma. The Council had come to a close and Bishop Reed was quite permissive in allowing his priests and people to implement the reforms of the Council. The very first document promulgated was *The Constitution on the Sacred Liturgy*. It stated clearly,

> *In the restoration and promotion of the sacred liturgy, the full and active participation by all the people is the aim to be considered before all else; for it is the primary and indispensable source from which the faithful are to derive the true Christian spirit."*

How about that for a mandate! Bill found himself in a parish located in a university town with an educated laity. He called to service two young and gifted liturgists, Gabe and Mary Jo Huck to design creative worship services. Remember, for the first time since the early days of Christianity, the liturgy was now celebrated in the people's language, English.

After an exciting three years in Norman, it seemed Bill Skeehan was ready for his own parish.

Resurrection Parish, Tulsa, 1968-1978

A group of creative women from three different parishes in Tulsa: St. Mary's, Magdalene, and St. Pius, were CCD teachers who were utilizing the biblical, liturgical, and catechetical reforms of the Council. In collaboration with their leader, Ginnie McCann, they contacted the diocesan Religious Education Office and stated they would like to move their Religious Education classes to their own homes. They formed eight Women's Guilds and developed a vibrant community among themselves.

When Father Bernard Jewitt, director of Tulsa's Religious Education office, became aware of the creative work they were doing, he suggested they might like to have a priest working with them. They asked Bishop Reed if a priest could assist them for a few hours per week. He responded that he was planning to establish a new parish in Tulsa in the very area where they were located.

Thus, it came about that Bishop Reed started two "experimental" parishes in 1968: John 23 in Oklahoma City led by Bill Nerin, and Resurrection Parish in Tulsa led by Bill Skeehan. The idea for experimental parishes, plus many more resolutions came out of the Diocesan Little Council that convened delegations from the entire diocese as a way to implement the changes that came from Vatican II.

When Father Bill arrived in Tulsa and held his first meeting with potential parishioners, he simply announced, "I have nothing. There is no church, no office. I don't even have a place to live." Truly, he was starting from scratch, and yet internally he felt up to the challenge. He was also aware that the parish actually came about from the initiative of a group of women who had gotten some assistance from Father Bernard Jewitt. Taking initiative like that impressed Bill and he would make use of that insight time and time again

John 23 had said that it was time for the church "to open some windows and let in some fresh air." In that same spirit, Bill Skeehan was aware that in starting an experimental parish, it would be his responsibility to lead in new directions and that it would often entail leading by listening to his people. He would learn from them.

Fundamental to Bill's notion of a church was his discovery of the significance of circles. Recall the diagram of the ecclesiology that came out of Vatican II, circular vs. that of a pyramid. There was no church building at Resurrection Parish. Fortuitously, the Tulsa Public School District allowed congregations that were on the way to building a church to use their school buildings for worship. In the geographical area of Resurrection was Memorial High School and the auditorium of Memorial became the setting for the celebration of the Eucharist. This was an ideal setting in which to arrange the chairs in a semi-circular fashion.

Without a church building, baptisms took place in the homes of parishioners. It worked out that the entry into the church community was also an entry into the neighborhood community. The baptism of an infant became an ecumenical activity, because half of the neighbors who attended were not Catholic.

We should point out that the Catholic population of Tulsa was at best about 8%. Catholicism in Oklahoma had a spirit of its own without a lot of the ecclesiastical trappings of more traditional Catholic areas of the United States.

One of the initial innovative things Bill did was to open a church office in the midst of a shopping center. Again, this setup attracted a mix of various kinds of people. A sign was placed on the front door that simply said "Resurrection." What was going on there, passers-by wondered – was this a "head shop"? Were they "peddling drugs"?

Eventually, Dan Allen, who was now pastor of a church on the north side of Tulsa, said to Bill, "I have just the right person for you." With that, in his inimitable way, Dan sent over an African American woman, Evelyn Jones, who was looking for a job. Mrs. Jones, better known simply as Evelyn, was a diamond in the rough.

She was the mother of twelve children and had spent most of her adult life working as a "domestic" on the more wealthy south side of Tulsa.

What to do with Evelyn – she couldn't read the phone book because she didn't know the alphabet. Bill saw that she had an opportunity to attend school for a couple of years and she began to take advantage of the opportunity and learned quickly. She learned typing and other secretarial skills and became a tremendous asset to the parish, not only as a secretary, but as "a jack of all trades." More people came to her for counseling than to the pastor.

Bill had some innate sense about the importance of words, finding appropriate words to express the meaning he wanted to convey. For example, in place of "committees", he used the term "ministries." Ministries would communicate a sense of who the members were, ministers who would carry out a function, whether it was the liturgy, prayer, or social justice ministry.

Deep within his psyche were also a sense of the sacred and the value of symbols. He wanted the people to understand the symbolism of baptism and how that sacrament is oriented to the Eucharist. "Remember, folks," he would say, "When you enter the church and bless yourself with holy water, it is a reminder of when you were initiated into the church through the water of baptism. So you bless yourself when you enter and participate in the Eucharist. Then, having been blessed that you might live the Eucharist in your daily life, it is not necessary to bless yourself when you leave the church."

Creating realistic symbols was a key to deepening the people's understanding of what was going on in the sacramental life of the church. The bread for the Eucharist had to look like bread, feel like bread in the hand, and taste like bread in the mouth. So the parish baked its own bread for their Eucharistic celebration.

The ministries were carried out in some 20 mini-parishes. This was another learning experience about the value of circles. Bill realized that when the members of a mini-parish sat in a circle, they tended to open up with one another and share what was going on in their lives.

The use of circles helped people to appreciate that they were all equals. Bill and Dan used circular seating in multiple situations. He recalled a gathering they had at the local YMCA. Dan had brought five people living in poverty in North Tulsa to the south section of the city. The five poor people were surrounded by a few concentric circles of lay people from Resurrection. The people in the inner circle presented situations they were confronted with on a daily basis: "I can't get my kids into good schools," etc., etc., and the lay people of Resurrection had no way of responding to their problems related to living in poverty. The evening turned into a valuable teaching-learning situation.

Once, while Bill and Dan were in New York City, they noticed an advertising campaign "Give a Damn for New York City" on posters throughout the city. Dan suggested that it would be a great slogan for Resurrection Parish. Thus "Give a Damn Sunday" was inaugurated. He had it put into parish bulletins and had "Give a Damn" lapel pins made for people to wear. Naturally the children and youth delighted in wearing the pin to shock their teachers. Through the campaign significant sums of money were raised to help the poor in Tulsa, especially the Neighbor for Neighbor program. In fact, Resurrection Parish began to pay the overhead for Neighbor for Neighbor including rent, utilities and salaries.

The influence of Dan Allen and the entire concept of Neighbor for Neighbor is immeasurable in terms of what Bill was putting into practice at Resurrection. The basic principle of Neighbor for Neighbor was as follows – if an individual or a family got help (such as car repairs, medical or dental help, employment, food, housing, legal advice, etc.) they, in turn, were to help someone else in need. Thus, the Social Justice Ministry at Resurrection had a variety of talented and skilled people doing volunteer work. They saved a whole neighborhood by repairing the sewers and replacing the pipes. They restored houses, and they also marched for civil rights and protested nuclear arms.

After a couple of years, when Memorial High School discovered that the members of Resurrection Parish did not have plans to build a church, they were politely told that they would have to make other plans for Sunday services. There happened to be a vacant church called The Church of God in their immediate area. Resurrection purchased the Church of God and it is still in use to this day. As they were preparing to move into their new building, Bill noticed an ad that an African-American Baptist Church in nearby Sapulpa was looking for pews. Resurrection removed the pews from their church, delivered them to the Baptists as a gift, and then purchased moveable chairs. They developed a multi-purpose room allowing them to use the space for whatever events they chose. In this way, even with a church building, the parish retained the flexibility they found so important whenever they gathered for an event.

Within two years of the birth of Resurrection, Bill began to reflect on what was happening in the parish. There was a growing sense of respect and trust developing not only between pastor and people, but also among and between the people themselves – individuals, couples, families were "getting it." They were getting a new awareness of what this mystery of Christ was all about. Bill couldn't help but notice that people were responding enthusiastically to his gospel-centered and social action directed homilies. Call it the grace of God, the influence of the Spirit; people were taking responsibility for their lives, their world in new ways.

Bill made an effort to keep other priests informed as to what was happening at the experimental parish and, sadly, most of those who responded favorably were those who later left the priesthood. The experience of many of the priests who left was that the promise of Vatican II was not being fulfilled and that struggle between change and renewal on the one hand and restoration of the old ways on the other was beginning to take place.

Yet through Bill's leadership, Resurrection was able to maintain an ecumenical sensitivity that God is present and active in all religions. There was an ever present tension between the amount of change the church can experience while still remaining faithful to its Tradition, and avoiding the "traditionalism" of the later centuries. With that tension came a continual call to conversion, both personal and institutional with the realization that the risen Christ is present and his Spirit guiding us.

In an interview with Jerry Jeep, one of the authors of this story, Bill seemed puzzled that some people were afraid of him, even bishops. Jerry helped Bill understand this reaction by putting it in the context of "Bill's own personal authority." He was confident and authoritative in himself and what he stood for. We recalled some volunteers had referred to him as a "loveable bear." He had a large frame and he could engulf a person in a warm embrace.

There was reason for optimism in the way things were progressing at Resurrection; parishioners were deepening in their understanding what was meant by a "preferential option for the poor," making their own decisions and acting on their own in a Christ-like manner. In the midst of that good will, February 17, 1971 occurred and launched an event that came to be known as the Warren Cathedral.

The Warren Cathedral

Joe Dillon was the elected priest's representative on the bishop's Pastoral Board. The board met on a weekly basis to determine diocesan policy. On the evening of date mentioned above, the pastoral board was to meet in Tulsa. Before Joe left for Tulsa from his residence in Oklahoma City, he received a phone call form Bill Skeehan and Dan Allen requesting that he meet with them prior to the board meeting. It seems that W. K. Warren, founder and owner of the Warren Petroleum Co., had written a letter to Bishop Reed with the generous offer to build a debt-free cathedral and chancery office in South Tulsa. Warren, a wealthy Catholic layman and member of Christ the King Parish, had already funded the building of a magnificent Catholic hospital, St. Francis Medical Center, in the area close to where the cathedral was to be built. What a plum for Bishop Reed!

But wait, there's more – a stipulation that Bill Skeehan would have to be removed as pastor, even though the parcel of land for the new cathedral would be located in Resurrection Parish. Let that sink in – as the Apostle Paul would say: "Had the Principalities and Powers been unleashed again?" or perhaps the evangelists: "the money changers have returned to the Temple."

The context is ever so interesting. Mr. Bill Warren had been a good friend of Bill's father. When Bill had celebrated his first Mass at Christ the King Parish in Tulsa, Mr. Warren was present. Following the Mass, Mr. Warren had knelt for Bill's blessing. Bill did not want to hurt Mr. Warren, but in conscience he knew he had to take a stand against the gift with a certain string attached. Bill also realized that the stand had to be from the parish as a whole, not from Bill alone. What were the odds that a 300-family parish could take on the power brokers of the diocese? Yet what Jesus of Nazareth was about in the gospels was at stake.

A fiery priest's representative, Joe Dillon, acting in the name of Bill, Dan and, as it turned out, the parish, took on the majority of the board. The bishop was somewhat taken aback – goodness, he couldn't have his priests against this project.

What did Mr. Warren have against Bill Skeehan? It seems it was a matter of four or five editorials in *The Tulsa World* newspaper that Bill had written concerning social justice issues in Tulsa. Perhaps it was as simple as "Give a Damn Sunday."

About a week after the board meeting, Bill was invited to appear as a guest on a TV talk show. You can imagine that Mr. Warren was not too keen on the publicity he was receiving. As a result of the attention that Bill had brought to the cathedral proposal, it was decided that a parish-wide meeting would be held at Bishop Kelley High School. The atmosphere was electric and you could cut the tension with a knife. Bishop Reed and Jack Sullivan, Episcopal Vicar for Tulsa spoke in favor of the gift to an overflow audience. Bill Skeehan and a layman from Resurrection Parish spoke against building a cathedral on their parish grounds. Parishioners were then asked to vote on the proposal and they rejected it by a 2/3 majority. Case closed!

Bill had made a counter-proposal that he and Resurrection would be willing to accept the cathedral if it came with a promise that a comparable amount of money would be made available to the citizens of North Tulsa (perhaps in the form of a decent medical facility). However, there were no takers on that deal.

A few days after the Kelley meeting, Bishop Reed invited Bill to lunch at his residence. The luncheon was quite civil. Perhaps somewhere in the back of his mind Reed knew that he was wrong in even considering that a layman could be in charge of personnel decisions simply because he disagreed with what Vatican II stood for.

Bill had sent a letter to the priests of the diocese stating his reasons for not accepting a gratuitous cathedral for the rich. He received little support from priests, who largely supported the bishop and a few angry responses.

Overall, it was a very courageous stand that Bill took, one of the most memorable moments of his priesthood. Bill celebrated the euphoria of the moment with a couple of priest friends by spending an overnight at a parishioner's cabin at Grand Lake. He was truly proud of the members of Resurrection parish for their grasp of what was at stake for the young parish and their willingness to make a Christ-like response with enthusiasm. Bill served at Resurrection for ten years and, in 1978, he agreed to exchange parishes with his friend, Father Bob Pickett, having survived two earlier efforts to have him removed as pastor.

The Idea of a Parish

What was the parish model that Bill and the people of Resurrection developed over a ten-year period and the model that Bill would take to his new assignment at The Community of St. James in Bartlesville?

A parish can be conceived of according to different models. A model is a particular way of thinking about the nature and purpose of a parish; it thus expresses that aspect of the parish one chooses to emphasize. Avery Dulles formulated five models or ways of considering a parish: as institution, as communion, as sacrament, as herald, as servant. The institutional model emphasizes the elements of leaders, laws, and teachings. Bill was choosing an institution with a thoroughly democratic structure rather than a monarchy. The communion model stresses the community of members united by a common belief and spirituality. The sacrament model focuses on how the parish makes the risen Christ present and active in the world. The herald model emphasizes the mission of the parish to preach the good news of Christ and to establish the kingdom of God. The servant model calls attention to the parish's role in transforming the immediate environment through service.

Editorial Note: the authors are adapting Dulles' five models of the church to a parish. *Models of the Church* (Garden City, NY: Image Books, 1987).

Though Vatican II supported all five of these models of church and parish, one of the council's major accomplishments was to shift the emphasis from the hierarchical institutional model to the communion model of the Church or parish forming a community in Christ. This was a monumental shift.

At Resurrection, and later at St James, the communion model was predominant. The parish is the People of God, a community utilizing a circular structure that emphasizes equality of each member. The sacrament model stressing baptism and eucharist was combined with the herald model through challenging gospel homilies calling listeners to action and opening them to the servant model in the spirit of Neighbor to Neighbor.

In the spirit of collegiality at the parish level, Vatican II had recommended the establishment of parish councils, by which the laity would share the decision-making in a parish with the pastor.

When a change in pastors at Resurrection Parish was under consideration, the parish council made a concerted effort to keep Father Skeehan as pastor. I am enclosing the letter to the bishop and the personnel board of the diocese together with the accompanying description of how the activities of the parish were organized under the direction of the Resurrection Parish Council. These documents are copied from the Skeehan Archives.

The spring of 1978

Most Rev. Eusebius J. Beltran
Chancery Office
Diocese of Tulsa
P.O. Box 2009
Tulsa, Oklahoma 74101

Dear Bishop Beltran:

To introduce you to Resurrection Parish, we are submitting this document prepared by the Parish Council over the past several months. It sets out the essence of what Resurrection is about in the Church and in the community. We believe Resurrection does much that is unique to communicate the message of Jesus in an urban environment.

This document is submitted for your consideration in connection with the personnel policies of the Diocese. It is our understanding that these policies provide for the transfer of a priest after a maximum period of ten years service in a parish. We urge exception to that policy in the case of Father Skeehan, and we believe the "Servant Message" of Resurrection under his leadership justifies an exception.

In the event that Father Skeehan must be transferred, we respectfully request the opportunity to be consulted during the selection process for the new pastor at Resurrection. For this reason, we are forwarding a copy of this letter and document to the Personnel Board of the Diocese.

Respectfully submitted

Tom L. Holland,
President for the Parish Council

Enclosure
c.c. Members of the Personnel Board; The Chancellor

CHURCH OF THE RESURRECTION

The Church of the Resurrection is a sacramental community of faith, professing the Lordship of Jesus Christ and dedicated to be a sign of the Kingdom on earth and an anticipation of the future Kingdom. Resurrection sees its mission in relationship to the Kingdom as threefold: to proclaim in word and sign that the Kingdom has come in Jesus; to offer itself as a test cast of its own proclamation by becoming a people transformed by the Spirit into a community of faith, hope, love and truthfulness – a community always struggling to create among its members prayerful, articulate and decisive persons; and to act with the pastor in shared responsibility, in the process of realizing and extending the Kingdom through service in the social, political and economic order. (Adapted from Richard McBrien, Church: The Continuing Quest, Newman Press).

The Pastor

A Pastor is:

1. a servant leader who:
    a. pursues a life-style integral with the preached word, simple, open and compassionate;
    b. avoids rule by fiat – recognizes the right of the pastor's veto, but ignores it in practice;

makes major decisions only in consultation with the Parish Council; plans, but only in the context of the parish ministries;

c. lets the fiscal responsibilities rest where they should, with the competent layperson and the ministry responsible for finances;

d. keeps people in touch with the larger Church, the needs of the Bishop and programs in other parishes.

2. a reflective, prayerful person who:

a. presides over parish celebrations with simplicity and respect for the roles of the lay ministers;

b. involves the people in the preparation of liturgies;

c. remains sensitive to the social, political, and economic issues in the secular community, and raises the consciences of the people in relation to these issues.

3. a listener who:

a. is obedient to the real needs of people within the parish and outside it;

b. is sensitive to the talents of parishioners assuming intelligence, creativity, imagination and faith among parishioners, allowing for spontaneity and giving them room to act creatively;

c. maintains contacts with the larger community, ministers, preachers of other faiths, the aged, the poor, those in power and the media people.

Ministerial Associate

The ministerial associate is:

1. a <u>partner of the pastor in the ministry of the Gospel</u> in a subordinate but collegial – not subservient – relationship. She/he shares the values, attitudes and direction of the pastor and parishioners to be served.

2. a <u>spiritual leader</u>:
   a. whose growing prayer life attunes her/him to the Spirit moving in the people and the people moving in the Spirit;
   b. who has deep reverence for each parishioner's responsibility to and gifts for participation in the priestly and prophetic ministry of Christ;
   c. who is available for individual as well as group personal needs.

3. a <u>resource person</u> for all the ministries, especially liturgy.:

Parish Council

The Parish Council of the Church of the Resurrection consists of seven members as follows: President; Vice-President; Administration Ministry Leader; Adult and Family Life Ministry Leader; Celebration Ministry Leader; Community Action Ministry Leader; and Intra-Parish Ministry Leader. The Pastor and the Ministerial Associate are ex-officio, non-voting members of the Council. The President and the Vice-President are elected from the parish at large for a term of one year. The ministry leasers are selected by the membership of the various ministries.

The Parish Council deliberates, formulates policy and advises the Pastor on all matters pertaining to the liturgical, financial, educational, and community affairs of the parish. The Pastor and the Parish Council share the responsibility of administering the parish and conducting the activities of the parish. Extensive responsibility for parish functions is delegated to the ministries. The needs of our parish are being met through this spirit of shared responsibility.

Administration Ministry

The Administration Ministry advises the Parish Council of the financial condition of the parish and, upon requests from the ministries, makes final budget recommendations to the Council. Fundraising for the parish is handled by this Ministry. The Ministry also provides the accounting and bookkeeping services needed by the Parish. Responsibility for maintaining the Church, its grounds and the office has been delegated to this Ministry. With the advice of this Ministry and the Pastor, the Parish Council makes major financial decisions for the Parish.

Adult & Family Life Ministry

The Adult and Family Life Ministry has the responsibility of fostering growth in faith within the family unit, the individual family member, and the single adult person.

Our direction in sharing the "good news" is focused on the community as adults. We believe that the primary responsibility for children's growth in faith rests with the parents.

To meet these responsibilities, we are committed to the following:

1. To be an extension of the pastoral message of Jesus Christ;
2. To encourage interaction in the community, as a body as well as in peer groups, through the presentation of theologically sound materials;
3. To foster the growth of Christian Community by providing experiences which will enrich and

strengthen that spirit as a commitment to all people;

4. To encourage personal growth through the presentation of specific materials which will meet the individual's needs.

Celebration Ministry

The purpose of the Celebration Ministry is to celebrate the goodness of life as reflected by Jesus Christ with language and symbols that express the faith experience of the Resurrection Community.

The Celebrant, supported by the Celebration Ministry, meets these needs by:

1. Supporting and bringing life to the liturgies of Resurrection Parish;
2. Being open to change in the composition of the parish, in the needs of the community and in the spiritual goals of Resurrection;
3. Supporting the education of the parish toward a richer understanding of the liturgical tradition of our faith.
4. Encouraging the community itself to celebrate non-sacramental liturgies in his absence;
5. Being comfortable with where we are now in our liturgies and where we want to go that we might grow together;

6. Striking a balance between dignity and hospitality, formality and spontaneity, and choreography and comfort;

7. having a deep feeling and sensitivity for symbol language that is the fruit of a long biblical and church tradition;

8. Viewing the Eucharistic celebration as the central, life-giving aspect of Resurrection Parish.

Community Action Ministry

We trust that the spirit of the Community Action Ministry is the spirit of Christ, the Servant. Like the followers of Jesus, we hope to minister to the immediate needs of the poor and suffering in the Tulsa community. Also, like the early Church, we hope to be professional "disturbers of the peace" – the false peace that so often lies over the community – by lending our voice to the poor, the oppressed and the discriminated against in our attempts to bring about those legislative and administrative changes that will reform our institutions that victimize.

With some understanding of Jesus as the Covenant uniting all men and women, we understand that ministry is not one of charity but of justice. We are daily enriched by the spirit of those whom we serve and those with whom we serve. We speak and work for change – not for change's sake – but only to effect hose changes in attitudes and structures which alone can bring about some small experience of the reign of the Spirit in our time.

Foremost among the organizations to which we are responding is Neighbor for Neighbor which is a movement – not an agency – to facilitate a dialog between the rich and the poor; to respond to the immediate needs of the poor and to educate the affluent; to change the economic and social structures that keep people in poverty. Others are: Bread for the World, Birthright, Meals on Wheels, Project-Get-Together, and Margaret Hudson School, to mention a few.

We, at Resurrection Church, need a pastor and ministerial associate who can help us keep foremost in our lives the Spirit of the Servant Christ.

Intra-Parish Ministry

Resurrection is divided geographically into nine mini-parishes in order to create smaller, more viable units where people can come to know each other and to respond to each others needs and the needs of the greater community. Mini-parishes provide a means for forming friendships, building communications and sharing responsibilities for the parish at large.

The Intra-parish Ministry is composed of Mini-Parish Coordinators and elected Intra-Parish Leaders (currently a couple who were formerly Mini-Parish Coordinators). The Intra-Parish Ministry meets the following needs: coming together as smaller communities; serving one another; providing hospitality; maintaining communication lines to the Parish at-large; and conducting intra-parish activities.

The Pastor and Ministerial Associate are integrally involved with all the mini-parishes and offer support and service to each of these groups.

In thus describing themselves and the structures of their interaction, the Resurrection parishioners were describing "What a Vatican II Parish Looks Like" as the title of this section suggests. In sum, Resurrection parish embodied these characteristics:

1. A Christian Community where the members know and care for each other and are united around the risen Christ and His Spirit.
2. Of the highest priority is an outstanding liturgy that stresses the people's full participation.
3. The people genuinely care about each other in their faith life and their human needs; for example, small groups, religious education, prayer, sacramental preparation, youth, the elderly and the sick.
4. The parish community reaches beyond itself to the larger community, particularly with reference to justice, poverty and peace issues.

The End of the Beginning

However, the die was cast; the bishop and the personnel board decided it was time for a new pastor. Bill Skeehan's departure from Resurrection coincided with the 10th anniversary celebration of the parish. A story in *The Eastern Oklahoma Catholic* (July 1978) described the celebration. Under the headline, "A Parish is the People not the Priest, Pastor says." Jacquie Harbour reported the words of Bill Skeehan to the parishioners:

> *This parish's greatness is exemplified in this evening's liturgy," he said. "It was done by you, and that is the way it should be."*
>
> *We have given you room to move…that's what this crazy religion is all about," he said. "The spirit moves because we try to be deeply human."*

Obviously moved by a letter he was handed just before Mass began, Father Skeehan shared the words of a little girl: "I love…I have loved you the four years I have been here…you gave me my First Communion, and you let me be an altar girl…I'll always remember you."

Beth Macklin, Religion Editor for *The Tulsa World*, entitled her article, "Founding Pastor Leaving Tulsa - Give a Damn Parish." We will quote from the lead-in the story. (*Tulsa World*, Friday, July 29, 1978)

What's going to *become of Tulsa's "Give a Damn"
Roman Catholic parish, Church of the Resurrection,
when the founding pastor, the Rev. William Skeehan,
leaves Tuesday?*

*"It will go right on being the giving, concerned-for
others parish it has been," predicted Skeehan, who will
move to St. James' Church, Bartlesville. "The parish is
the people, not the priest, but I believe the Rev. Robert
Picket (coming from St. Cecilia's Church, Claremore,
to serve Resurrection parish) will encourage the
parishioners to continue the kind of spirit we have
established."*

*Resurrection parishioners will gather at 7:30 pm
Friday at Memorial High School, where the parish's
first mass was celebrated by Skeehan, for his final mass
as their pastor, and to observe the parish's 10th
anniversary. The service originally was planned for the
school cafeteria, site of the first mass, but the parish
has grown to such an extent (543 families), the
auditorium will be needed to house the more than 1,000
persons expected.*

*Every family has been asked to bring flowers to
decorate the room. It is typical of Resurrection
parishioners that arrangements have been made
following the service to distribute the flowers to nursing
home residents. The aim of Resurrection Parish from
its outset has been to share themselves – their time,
talents and money – with other people, rather than
spending on "bricks and mortar."*

The parish's annual contributions are in excess of $100,000, a great chunk of which goes to support Neighbor for Neighbor, a group which depends on community support for its private fight on poverty in Tulsa, and similar organizations.

"We had $13,000 on hand last Sunday," Skeehan said, "so we divided it among the Margaret Hudson program, Sunshine Services (both cut back in recent Community Development grants by the city), and some other programs we think are worthwhile."

He estimates Resurrection parishioners have given far in excess of $100,000 to Neighbor for Neighbor, directed by former Catholic priest Dan Allen, a longtime friend of Skeehan.

"We gave them over $30,000 last year alone." That's when NFN's treasury was hard-hit paying gas bills so that poverty-stricken Tulsans could remain warm during the excessively cold winter of 1976-77.

"Give a Damn" is over and above contributions to the parish budget," Skeehan explained. Resurrection parishioners started "Give a Damn" four years after the church's beginning, taking the name from a poster which hangs behind Allen's desk.

This fund, based on quarterly giving by parishioners (they were asked to give $3 a month per family) is designed to guarantee the low wages paid NFN staffers.

Skeehan will leave Resurrection under a diocesan rule that priests may serve a parish for only ten years. "Going will be "traumatic," he told his parishioners, "because it has been my life, and not just another assignment." In an interview, he said founding and forming the parish "has been the greatest experience of my life."

It was established to serve the area between 41st and 51st streets and Hudson and Yale avenues, but the parish's south boundary presently is 81st Street and it extends east to Garnett Road."

40 Years Later, 1968-2008

During the year 2008, Resurrection parish celebrated its 40th anniversary. The commemoration involved the making of two DVDs in which a number of the parishioners who were on hand from the very beginning were interviewed as they recalled what their experience was like. The five priests who had served as leaders of the faith community were also given the opportunity to share their experiences. One of the amazing things that came out of the interviews was how the spirit Resurrection parish started with, under Bill Skeehan, had been retained over the years.

We have already covered most of the stories that go back to Bill Skeehan himself except for what others said about him and their experience. A question was raised, "How did you find out about Resurrection?"

One source was Jim McNamee, the Pastor at Madeline parish. Jim McNamee was considered the oracle of the diocese. He was a well-read, learned theologian who wrote letters frequently to the local newspaper on a variety of current topics.

When asked about Resurrection, Father Jim would respond: "Oh, you ought to go there; Bill Skeehan is the best homilist in the diocese." One man spoke up and said, "We considered Bill to be the spiritual heir of Jim." Several of the people present said, "We went to Mass there and we liked it. We like the spirit of hospitality that existed there." Many respondents said they were impressed by the liturgical celebrations – "they touched your heart as we were learning about the emphasis on the Liturgy of the Word that came from Vatican II."

One man piped up and said: "The first time I went to Mass at Resurrection, I asked myself was this really a Catholic church? I kept coming back, however, and before long my thought was – this is the way every Catholic Church should be."

There was a spirit at Resurrection: "We are one, we are family. We had a free-flowing parish council that was concerned with social action, responding to the real needs of people." You could see it – people's lives were changing." Now get this – "At the end of the year, whatever money we had, we gave to Neighbor for Neighbor, year after year."

Father Bill Hamill, OSA – Bill Skeehan took a medical leave because of an ailing back during part of 1972-73, and Fr. Hamill filled in on many Sundays. These are Fr. Bill Hamill's impressions:

"Having the opportunity to help out at Resurrection was a significant event in my life. I was impressed with how well Bill knew everyone in the parish and even the details of their lives, like the names of all their children. Tulsa was blessed to have such a parish as an option to participate in. The creativity of the Liturgy and the Social gospel collaboration with Neighbor for Neighbor added to the quality of life in the Tulsa community. Naysayers referred to it as 'Insurrection parish.' I don't think you could establish such a parish today."

This last remark is a sad commentary on how much the restoration movement in the Church, at all levels, has replaced the spirit of renewal from Vatican II.

1978-1997, Father Bob Pickett – He succeeded Bill as the second pastor at Resurrection. As a close friend of Bill's, he continued what Bill had started. In a brief reflection, he said: "From the beginning I was impressed with the spirit of the Parish and how active the laity was in planning well-thought out liturgies." Bob Pickett continued the active collaboration with Dan Allen and Neighbor for Neighbor. He spoke of his friendship and admiration for Dan, "so generous indeed, one of a kind."

1997-2005, Father Mike Knipe – He was touched with "the simplicity, service, and intimacy of Resurrection; it was a fun parish." He saw the parish "as continuing to grow strong and reach out." As the demographics of the population in Tulsa changed, "resurrection accepted and embraced Latinos in their midst; I am grateful that I served as pastor."

2005 – to the Present, Father Steve Austin – "I had a great admiration for Bill Skeehan and Resurrection Parish from the moment I was ordained. I am impressed with the vibrant music at our celebrations. The people like to gather in informal settings as they plan their ministries, visiting the sick at hospitals and nursing homes."

When asked to name three qualities that stand out most at Resurrection, Austin replied. "Three qualities are the style of worship, the hospitality, and the ministry to those in need. It has been an honor and pleasure to serve as pastor these last four years."

As the first Director of Religious Education, Mary Minden recalled for Bill her three-year experience working at Church of the Resurrection. *You took me that evening to the home of Ginny McCann to meet some of the women (maybe a few men) who had actually started the parish. They would be among the teachers in the religious education program. In fact, they had already begun teaching. This was not a church reaching out to the people. The people had gone to the bishop. It was men and women bringing the community to the church and requesting they be recognized as a parish stating their need for and requesting a priest. No, I did not comprehend all that in the first meeting with you or with the women. However, I was immediately impressed with your amazement and excitement about the people taking the initiative. I knew a few priests who appreciated what parishioners were doing, but this was unique. You respected and valued them and what they were accomplishing. They accepted you as their leader, but actively participated with ideas and questions. It was only the beginning of my awareness of the community as Church.*

"There were no buildings and really no discussion of future buildings. The office was to be in a store front, classes in homes and for Sunday mass we would rent space in the public high school. Later, we would rent or be allowed to use space in other public buildings for adult education and group activities for children. I quickly began to share your amazement and excitement as the unique parish continued to form and grow.

"I recall you explaining to me the choice of the name of the parish and of the logo you designed. It was not Resurrection Church but Church of the Resurrection. It

was the church of the living Christ, Christ living among us. And that was what was written across the logo in block letters: Church of the Resurrection ...Jesus Lives!

"It was a vibrant parish. Today we hear requests for volunteers or laments that not enough parishioners come forward to serve. At Resurrection, there seemed to be a wealth of volunteers. You, Evelyn, and I were the staff and there was a parish council, but we had so many people who came regularly to serve in whatever capacity was needed. Jim was hired for the music, but he mentioned Sunday that Bernie Bartlett was the first organist...another example of a volunteer when needed. Again, that brings home that it was the people, the community of the church. And you were so much a part of that community, not set apart. You were personal, involved, and a friend. Bill, you are not going to get around the place you had in the story of this parish. You drew people together, inspired, challenged, laughed and shared in personal disappointments and sorrow. You made us uncomfortable in a way that prompted action. GIVE A DAMN Sunday was a wake-up call. Look at all the personal involvement in Neighbor for Neighbor, the social issues...the Church of the Resurrection, as I knew it in its early beginnings, was evidence of God's grace in action. And so it continued.

"I remember the hours we spent on banners...for the office and the liturgy. What more can I say about that...just lots of good memories.

"My first Holy Week there was an awakening for me. Christ suffering now...Christ present now...Christ living now among us. Good Friday is the most memorable. Come to think of it, you didn't have all the services, but Friday was definitely about social consciousness, awareness of Christ suffering today. This related to what I said earlier. The people learned to get outside their personal comfort zone and live the gospel message."

St. James, Bartlesville, 1978-2004

Having thwarted two previous attempts by the diocesan powers that be to remove him as pastor of Resurrection Parish, Bill Skeehan agreed to leave provided that his friend, Bob Pickett, would replace him. And so it came about that Bill went to the Community of St. James in Bartlesville, and Bob to Resurrection Parish in Tulsa.

At this point, it might be helpful to give a short history of the St. James Parish Fr. Bill had inherited. For many years St. John's had been the lone Catholic Church in Bartlesville. It was led by Rev. John F. Lynch as pastor. In 1961, St. John's completed the construction of a new church building. Since the St. John's Catholic school was at a capacity enrollment, Father Lynch purchased some property on Douglass Lane which would be the location for St. Jude's school.

Construction of the school began in early 1964 and it was estimated that the new school would open for the 1965-66 school year. When Bishop Reed became aware that the new school was being built, he decided that it would be best that St. Jude's School would become the beginning of a whole new parish, to be called St. James.

Father Robert Pickett was appointed as the first pastor. The first Mass was celebrated on August 29, 1965 with formal dedication ceremonies for both church and school held on December 6, 1966. The school operated for three years with three Ursuline sisters from Paola, Kansas, serving as principal and faculty. After the first year, there were only two nuns available and a lay teacher was hired. The school had three classrooms, each housing two grades. When the Ursuline sisters could supply only one sister, it was no longer financially feasible to continue the school. St. James's school was closed prior to the school year of 1969-70.

Bob Pickett was a close friend of both Bill Skeehan and Dan Allen, and the trio spent many Mondays off together at their rustic cabin. Since Bob came to St. James about the same time that the Council in Rome ended, he was the first pastor responsible for bringing the spirit of Vatican II renewal to Bartlesville. He lined up a series of stimulating adult education classes conducted by the diocesan Religious Education Office. Bob was also a "true ham" at heart and would stage an annual dramatic production performed by parishioners.

In February, 1973, Tulsa became a diocese and Bernard J. Ganter was appointed the first bishop. One year later, Bob Pickett was transferred from St. James to St. Cecelia's in Claremore, Oklahoma, which was known as the childhood home of one of Oklahoma's favorite sons, Will Rogers.

The replacement for Bob Pickett as pastor came in the person of Fr. Frank Warnke, a priest of a somewhat more traditional background. It was an awkward situation for both priest and people. Fr. Warnke was used to a more authoritarian model in which the pastor was the decision-maker, whereas the parishioners had been introduced to a more collegial model of Vatican II. It was said that Fr. Warnke did mellow while at St. James.

During the last two years of Fr. Warnke's tenure at St. James, a fortuitous financial development took place. A nearby public school, Ranch Heights Elementary School, needed temporary facilities while a major expansion of their school building was under construction. A rental agreement was worked out with St. James for Ranch Heights students to use the parish's vacant classrooms. At about the same time, the property on Tuxedo Blvd., which St. James had inherited from St.

John's, was sold. The income from the classroom rental, the sale of the Tuxedo property, plus the generosity of St. James parishioners enabled the parish to retire the original debt of $200,000.

In the fall of 1978, Bill Skeehan replaced Frank Warnke as pastor, and in doing so, Bill stepped into a unique situation – a Catholic parish that was not only solvent, but even had some money in the bank. What an opportunity for someone like Bill, who believed that financial resources were to be used for the needs of the community.

Bob Pickett had provided the initial leadership for the active participation of the laity, not only in the church itself, but also to the community of Bartlesville. As Bill Skeehan built on that vision, the name of the parish was changed to The Community of St. James. The purpose of the change was obvious – this was not merely a parish of Catholics, but a Community that is at the service of those in need in Bartlesville and beyond.

The scene is some 13 years since the close of the Second Vatican Council. Since the spirit of renewal that flowed from Vatican II was at the heart of what Bill Skeehan brought to his priestly ministry and the parishes he served, it is important that we review some of the principles enunciated by the Council.

The document called the <u>Dogmatic Constitution on the Church</u> was the centerpiece of the Council. It brought forth a "new" ecclesiology or theology of church as mystery, as the people of God, as sacrament of the risen Christ and of our salvation. In a certain sense, the other documents depend on this teaching and are a further development of it.

Key passages communicated a new understanding of church which entailed the following characteristics:

1. The church is described as the people of God, primarily a community of persons. Recall how important it was for Bill that the people interacted in a circular formation.

2. "When I came to the church in Bartlesville (St. James), I saw immediately that it was a square building originally built as a school. Rather than using it the long way, I turned it sideways, so that now everyone in the church could see me and each other.

   "When we celebrated weekday Masses in the chapel, we took the chairs to the front and formed them into a circle where we discussed the scripture readings. Then we formed another circle around the altar. So we had two circles, a liturgy of the Word circle and a liturgy of the Eucharist circle. It was a powerful experience for the people.

   "The Liturgy of the Word became like a *lectio divina*, in which those present reflected as a group on the meaning of the Scripture readings for us today. The prayerful meditation led to compassion for those in need, so that the Eucharist was lived.

3. The constitution on the church emphasized the dignity, equality, and mission of the non-ordained in the church – called by God to the fullness of Christian life and love.

4. The church is not identical with the kingdom of God. So it's possible to appreciate other religions and all people of good will.

5. The Roman Catholic Church is not identified exclusively with the church founded by Christ. This called for participation in the ecumenical movement and radically changed the notion that "outside the church there is no salvation."

The Pastoral Constitution on the Church in the Modern World redefined the description of the church's mission and work, and what it means to be a Catholic in today's world, with emphasis on the church's social teaching and its commitment to social justice.

The Constitution on the Sacred Liturgy called for a complete revision of all the liturgical rites and provided Catholics with a new experience of worship and of a spirituality based on the Bible.

The basic principles of the above mentioned documents (...*Modern World* and ...*Liturgy*), were lived par excellence at St. James. From the very beginning, there was an emphasis on the community celebration of the sacraments, Baptism and the Eucharist. St. James also used moveable chairs placed in a circle and a multi-purpose room to gather people for a variety of events. The parish made excellent use of colorful and meaningful banners that accompanied their celebrations. The creative banners were made under the direction of Mike Calnan.

First Communions were a family affair. Each child made First Communion when the family decided that the child was ready. At the time, for the reception of the sacrament of Confirmation, a rite of passage to a more responsible role in the community, Bill would take each candidate aside and in his friendly manner, would ask: "Is this what you want for yourself or is this what your parents want for you"? This celebration of maturation in the faith was to be the person's own decision.

Those responsible for planning the liturgical celebrations would use innovative ways to intensify participation for special occasions. For example, on Ash Wednesday, at the time for distribution of the ashes, the whole family or a group would go up and receive the ashes from Fr. Skeehan and bring them back and place the ashes on other members of the family or group. On Holy Thursday, the entire community was seated at small round tables and one member at each table would receive the sacred bread and wine and then distribute it to the other participants around the table.

One Holy Thursday, after the Blessed Sacrament had been transferred to the altar of repose, a woman rose and spontaneously began to dance. Soon the entire congregation formed a line of dancers weaving in and out among the tables. It so fit the celebration, that the dance became a tradition added to the ritual for Holy Thursday.

Long ago, Bill realized that the washing of feet on Holy Thursday was an anachronism. We don't live in a dusty terrain nor do we wear sandals, but what the washing of the feet symbolized, the notion of service, was extremely important. So at each Holy Thursday celebration, a list of community organizations that needed volunteers was passed out and members of the parish would make their commitment for the coming year.

Music Ministry

Mike Calnan was the Music Director during the time Father Bill was at St. James. He is an unusually gifted person with music. He spoke of how much Bill trusted him to be in charge of selecting and arranging the music. "He allowed me to use my own creativity and, over the years, I learned to read the Sunday Scripture readings in the way that he did. In this way, we developed a marvelous synchronicity between the homily and the music for the day. Bill Skeehan so embodied *sacramentalilty* that the community became the sacrament.

Lay Leadership

Bartlesville was exceptional for a small town or city in Oklahoma in that it was the home base for the Phillips Petroleum Corporation, founded by Frank Phillips. As a result, the community had a plethora of well-educated professional people, many of whom were Catholic from other parts of the U.S. This provided St. James with a remarkable talent pool to draw from for any number of ways to serve. It was somewhat late in Bill's tenure at St. James that the top echelon of Phillips executives moved their headquarters to Houston. This loss, however, did not seem to diminish the quality of the lay leadership at the parish.

In establishing a parish council Bill clearly explained that this was a lay ministry and that the members would be in charge. "The decisions that you make will guide the activities of the parish. Even though we may not be in full agreement, I will never exercise a veto of any decision." Bill further empowered the council with this bit of wisdom from his own fertile mind: "The decisions you arrive at will determine the kind of church you want. The budget is your theology," said Bill.

The decisions of the parish council, together with the cooperation of a group of spirited parishioners, has created an outstanding example of what a Vatican II Parish would look like with an assortment of outreach activities to the larger community. As an outstanding example, we are including an article from the Bartlesville newspaper:

Bartlesville Examiner-Enterprise
Sept. 18, 1978

Alternative HS gets $10,000 rent donation

Bartlesville's St. James Parish has decided to donate up to $10,000 to the Alternative High School it was announced at the school's Wednesday advisory council meeting.

Father Bill Skeehan said the parish council decided to support the school for dropouts by donating up to $10,000 of the school's $31,000 budget. The advisory council, which has sought funds from the Oklahoma Crime Commission, Bartlesville's business sector, civic organizations and the Bartlesville school board had amassed $18,000 prior to Thursday's announcement.

The Bartlesville Public School System is renting classroom space (at St. James Elementary School) to the tune of $26,000 a year. "What we're simply doing is returning $10,000 of it," Skeehan told the council. "The donation," Skeehan explained, "will be a minimum of $3,000 with a possible $7,000 more if the *school needs the funding to reach its $31,000 projected budget."*

"If less than $7,000 is needed to meet the budget, then the corresponding amount will be donated," Skeehan told the council.

The school was started in January of this year but has been in financial trouble since it was originally funded by a grant by the Oklahoma Crime Commission. The purpose of the school is to encourage students who have either dropped out or have been expelled to reenter school

Emphasis is on individualized instruction to meet the academic and personal needs of the students. Proponents of the school bill it as an opportunity for the dropout to reenter mainstream society.

The school was housed on the Tri-County Tech campus earlier this year but will probably be housed in the old civic center this year.

In addition to filling academic gaps, the curriculum encourages the students to seek a vocational career, employment or higher education.

"All the students who finished the program this year are back in school," said Barbara Tillman, a council member who counsels juveniles.

Many citizens in the Bartlesville community appreciated the leadership as well as the generosity exercised by St. James. In turn, the lay members of the

Community of St. James felt empowered by the reception they received. Besides the money that was donated, several parishioners were involved in the remodeling of the building that became the school.

Earlier in our account of Father Bill's time at Resurrection Parish in Tulsa, we mentioned his connection to the Neighbor for Neighbor program started by his good friend Dan Allen. Bill Skeehan brought that same love for and dedication to N for N to his parishioners at St. James. We will quote from the "Remarks" that Bill spoke at the 20th anniversary of the Neighbor for Neighbor Free Clinic, June 22, 1991.

In the Gospel of Saint John we read:

The Word became flesh; he came to dwell among us…through him all things came to be; no single thing was created without him. All that came to be was alive with his life, and that life was the light of humankind. The light shines on in the dark, and all the darkness has never quenched it…

We have, of course, ever since then, made frantic and deliberate efforts to change flesh back into words. Words, words, words. Words from scholars - words from politicians - words from preachers - words, words, words. We have, through a blizzard of words, denied the incarnation. The Word became <u>flesh</u>…." The Word did not become word - the Word became flesh…the word came to <u>dwell</u> among us - to live - to *abide - to fully enter the human condition…and since that <u>Final</u> Word of God is risen and lives, then that Word still becomes flesh, still abides in us. But, unfortunately, we have reduced the Word to words. We have taken his flesh from him…and dry bones remain.*

It reminds me of the story in the gospels about Jesus restoring life to Jairus' daughter. Jesus, in the midst of the wailing and moaning, clamor and din, restores the child to life: "Little girl, get up." And then He says an astonishing thing: "Give her something to eat." We would have said: "Take her to church to pray." we who are more spiritual than God. The incarnation (<u>incarno</u> - taking flesh), "the Word-becoming-flesh", is untheological, unsophisticated, undignified … absurd …madness. It is <u>we</u> who have made it theological, sophisticated, dignified, logical, sane, by reducing the Word to words, to dogmas, to propositions, to creeds.

The prophets of old were preludes - precursors to the Word of flesh. <u>Amos</u>: "How serious your sins! Oppressing the just - accepting bribes - repelling the needy at the gates." Words of flesh. <u>Isaiah</u>: "the fasting that I wish is: releasing those bound unjustly - setting free the oppressed - sharing your bread with the hungry - sheltering the homeless - clothing the naked… <u>then</u> your light shall break forth like the dawn … otherwise you live in darkness." Words of flesh.

Jesus, the final Word, at the beginning of His public life, stood up in his home town synagogue and delivered

His inaugural address, Words of flesh: "I have been sent to bring glad tidings to the poor ... to proclaim liberty to captives ... recovery of sight to the blind..."

Later on in His public life, at one of his press conferences, called the Sermon on the Mount, Jesus made a policy statement about a "new world order." Blest are the poor, the reign of God is yours. Blest are you who hunger, you shall be filled. Blest are you who are weeping, you shall laugh. It is we who have de-fleshed these words by seeing in them rewards by and by in the sky when we die.

Finally, at the end of His public life, Jesus delivered his "state of the Kingdom" address: "For I was hungry and you gave me food. I was thirsty and you gave me drink. I was a stranger and you welcomed me, naked and you clothed me. I was ill and you comforted me." Words of flesh.

Where do we think these people still meet the Word... in a church? At a revival? On evangelical television?

The poor meet the Word-made-flesh when they meet us. The poor have been meeting the Word in North Tulsa for 20 years - not just words, but the Word-made-flesh. They meet the Word when they sit across the desk from you at in-take. Funny word, in-take. Incarnation: taking flesh. Taking in that poor person - unconditional personal regard for that person - the whole person, flesh and blood, at that very moment. The poor meet the Word through the interviewer who details the prescription needs, who does it with gentleness and warmth...creating a kinder, gentler ambience for the sick. The poor meet the Word through the nurse's loving touch - the nurse who makes no judgments about the patients clothes...of smell or lice in the scalp. The poor meet the Word through the competence, sense of humor and serious care of those filling the prescriptions...words on paper take in flesh in medicine. The poor meet the Word through the doctor whose skilled hands, intelligent mind, and gentle heart, listens well and responds with compassion. The poor meet the Word through the medical technician who patiently and carefully test the body fluids.

The Word doesn't float somewhere in midair. The Word needs flesh to act, to reach out, to touch...and the only flesh the Word has around is ourselves. Ourselves – not just because we volunteer, not just because we are there as nurses or doctors or welcomers, but because of our personal, real presence to that particular poor person...we are the body and blood of Christ in that deeply human meeting.

There are two corollary mysteries involved here: Death and Resurrection, flowing out of and completing the mystery of the incarnation. These, too, must take flesh - become real and present...or they, too simply remain words! Theological gobble-de-gook. We enter these mysteries when we freely give flesh to the Word, for to give flesh to the Word is to die a bit to ourselves and, thereby, be life-giving to another. To reach out, to touch, to embrace, to heal the poor, demands a gift of my time, my talents, my resources to the other, for the other. Which is translated: Incarnation / Death / Resurrection / the Neighbor for Neighbor Clinic.

The idea of social justice at St James is not simply to give a hand-out to people; rather social justice is exemplified by the economic development program brought to life by Susan Murphy. (Susan asked that we would not single her out, but we didn't know how to tell the sewing machine story without doing so.) Laura Summers relates what happened some eight years ago and continues to happen through the project known as Martha's Task.

Sewing Work Keeps Lives from Unraveling

By Laura Summers
World Correspondent

BARTLESVILLE – Gwen Ogans says she could have ended up on the streets. Instead, she's just completed contract work sewing microwave cooking pouches for a customer in Alaska.

The journey from poverty to running a business begins for Ogans and others at Martha's task, where low-income women learn to sew and sell their wares.

"If it weren't for this, I know I could be on the streets. I know what could've happened," Ogans said.

Susan Murphy, Martha's Task director, was among the founders of the organization which has for eight years been working to break the cycle of poverty with the help of donated sewing machines, thread and yards of colorful material.

It began for Murphy in the Catholic church, where a priest inspired her to find a way to help the poor.

Murphy, who ironically enough does not know how to sew, has seen the project develop from a tiny room in the basement of St. John Catholic Church to the storefront and workroom at 718 S. Johnstone Ave., where classes are held Monday through Thursday.

Aprons, pillow cases, designer purses and baby bibs are sold in the Sew Original store on the site, open from 9 a.m. to 2 p.m. weekdays. More than 200 women have benefited from Martha's Task through the years.

Martha's Task provides an economic development program with long-term education in sewing, marketing and retail.

Women are provided with everything they need to sew the items stocked in the store.

Once they develop their skills to an independent level, the women are given sewing machines and lighting for their homes, so they can expand the work.

There is also an emergency assistance branch of the program that allows women to obtain immediate cash for needs like prescriptions, food or rent payments. The women participating in the short term crisis intervention sessions make cards and crafts that often require no sewing, which gives them a way to earn money quickly.

Carolina Parsons came to Martha's Task five years ago with limited sewing skills, but now she's earning money and winning prizes for her handiwork at the county fair.

"I've had some good teachers through the years," Parsons said. "I can make all kinds of things."

Murphy loves seeing the sense of ownership the women have in the program. Some of the women banded together into a group, calling themselves "Martha's Girls" and have applied for the grant that could fund keeping the store open longer hours so they can do more work.

The organization and its seamstresses also have developed contract work where customers can choose fabric and ask to have a purse or apron made a certain way.

Customers from as far away as Alaska and New York have purchased items from members trained by the nonprofit.

Murphy said the program was named after St. Martha, the patron saint of servants and cooks, who is often depicted as a barefoot woman standing on top of a dragon.

Some twenty years into Bill's time with The Community of St. James, another social action project was launched through the efforts of five people with an abundance of creative imagination, Mary Martha Outreach known as MMO. The five instigators were Jaime and Ovia Wood, Mary Hudson, and Gertrude and Cliff Sousa; their starting date was October 1, 1998.

We will simply copy one page from the MMO Newsletter that shows the MMO First Quarter Statistics for 2009. It will give the reader some understanding of the comprehensive approach of this program.

MMO First Quarter Statistics 2009

Food

- Pantry fed a total of 8,091 people in 2,455 families (736 new people in 254 families) this quarter.
- During the quarter, 2,455 individual families came in one time totaling 8,091 people. (For the total quarterly count, each individual family (2,455) came in weekly totaling 17,667 people.)
- Out of the 8,091 people:
  - Children and youth total 3,001 or 37%
  - Seniors over 55 years of age total 1,337 or 17%
  - People between ages 18-54 total 3,753 or 46%
  - Single parents 911
  - Out of the 8,091 people, 1,618 are physically or mentally disabled, 20%

MMO purchased 106,959 lbs. of food from the Tulsa Community Food Bank

MMO received 4,350 lbs. of food from other sources.

MMO received 80% of the food from vendors of Wal-Mart food distribution center totaling 111,904 lbs.

Therefore, MMO gave out a total 227,563 lbs. or (114 tons of food) to clients this quarter.

MMO Food Distribution team gave away 20% or 27,976 lbs. of the Wal-Mart DC food to other agencies' orders).

Pantry volunteer hours totaled 2,708.

Community Garden hours total 71

Total Volunteer Hours for food is 2,708

Clothing

Garments given away totaled 55,581

Shoes – 2,096 pairs

Total Volunteer hours for Clothing is 809

Crisis

Monthly Sundries were given out to 1,010 families.

Total Sundry hours 317

Haircuts – 120

Crisis Room helped 263 families with household items.

Burnouts – 3

Shelter -1

Furniture – 148 families

Diapers – 4 pallets given to clients of MMO, Concern, Family Planning and Birthright.

Diapers were given to 294 clients
Wal-Mart products distributed from UW of Bentonville
- 16 pallets valued at $24,300 year-to-date
Total Crisis volunteer hours are 873
Total Crisis families helped 2,211
Total Volunteer hours for the 3 programs for 1st Quarter
is 5,747 from 127 Volunteers

MARY MARTHA OUTREACH WORK CREW REPORT – APRIL, 2009

Jail crews worked all four weekends in April, 102 hours in the garden, 52 hours in clothing and garage sale, and 7 more hours in the pantry, for a total of 161 hours. 18 new inmates participated this month in addition to those who have worked previously.

Total hours worked are now 177 in the garden, 64 in the pantry and 52 in the clothing/garage sale areas for a total of 293 hours in three months. 43 different individuals have now participated, and crews have ranged in size from 5 to 13. Total of 11 weekends worked out of a possible 13 since the start of the program.

In addition to all the general labor supplies by the crews, we have had tree trimmers who took care of pruning all of the trees on the property, professional painters who have worked on the various shelves, a carpenter who did some furniture repair for us, and now two who can best be described as "Jacks of all trades" who have done wonders in getting all of our broken down mechanical equipment working again. I've really enjoyed working with all of them.

Fred Morris
Garden Manager and Pantry Co-Chairman

Two other essential components of the Community of St. James Outreach to the larger community of the Bartlesville area were: 1) Green Free Clinic – founded by Cindy Pribil – The Clinic included three programs: Primary Care Services, Patient Assistance Program, and Mental Health and Chronic illness; 2) Eldercare started by Betty Summer. The Eldercare program has grown to an umbrella group serving some 1,000 seniors in the Washington and Nowata Counties.

While composing the brief summary of the Outreach to the larger community, it was documented that, during the 26-year ministry of Father Bill, the Community of St. James contributed cash in the amount of $1 million dollars.

The policy developed by the volunteers who participated in the Outreach had three basic operating principles:

1. Never simply say "No" to a person's request. See if there is some need that can be met.
2. Never charge a fee for our services.
3. Respect the dignity of each person making a request.

At one point in our discussion with Bill, he related a personal anecdote which provides a picture of how well he related to the larger Bartlesville community:

"A judge whom I knew quite well called me and said that another judge was dying and that at one time she had been a Catholic. My friend suggested that I visit her. I followed up the call with several visits. In the process of talking to her, I explained that she had not really left the church, but that the church had left her. She decided that she would like to remain in communion with the church.

It turned out that she was a well-known and respected judge, and after she died, the funeral procession went clear to Dewey, three miles out, two cars across, patrolled by police cars with flashing lights. Since St. John's Church was the only place large enough to hold the crowd that would attend, I asked to hold the funeral service there. Of the 600 plus people that would attend the service, perhaps only 20-40 would be Catholic.

Having consulted my wisdom box, I knew that a Catholic Mass would be out of place for that congregation. Instead, I conducted a scripture service with three readings and after each reading there was an appropriate response. The agenda had been printed, so the community present could respond and pray together. I concluded the service with a brief homily.

As I was leaving the Church, an older lady approached me and said: "Father, I've been going to Catholic Masses for 40 years and this is the first one I ever understood." And Bill chuckled at the memory.

Toward the end of our interview with Bill, he described himself succinctly in these words: "I'm not a theorist, not a theologian, I'm a preacher." Perhaps we should say he is truly a superb homilist. So much so, that a number of persons in the community of St. James referred to as "the Meddlers" convinced him to let them publish his homilies in what became three books.

The first book of homilies was entitled, *To Dance with a Cross on Our Back: Reflections on the Word Make Flesh* (1998). The **Preface** is as follows:

The making of this book was inevitable. For many years, parishioners and visitors alike have requested copies of Father Skeehan's homilies. He has a gift that enables him to make Scripture come alive and take root in our lives. Soon the idea of a book was born – born not by Father Bill, but by those to whom he ministers. While copies of homilies eventually became easy to obtain, the agreement to publish his works in book form was much later in coming.

More than a year ago, a group of women began "meddlin.' Things soon began to fall in place and eventually Father Bill agreed to this project. We began with this mission statement:

With the hope of inspiring all people of faith to meditate on the integral relationship between Scripture and life in this century, we have come together to compile a collection of Father Bill's writings which will reflect his Christ-inspired vision, philosophy, and personality. In doing so, may our efforts reach out, through his poetic voice, to draw our circle, our St. James family and our extended community into deeper communion with each other and, ultimately, with God.

With a short schedule, ambitious hands and the help of the Holy Spirit, we have reached this milestone. This book is a gift to all who want the Word to take hold of their hearts and their lives. (5, 7-8, back cover)

CIRCLE 4 MEDDLERS - THE COMMUNITY OF ST. JAMES

"What keeps us from despair, what keeps us as a people of hope in the Christian paradox, is that He who is to come is already here. He is in our midst...That is why, within our frailty, we can do the unimaginable:

WE CAN DANCE WITH A "CROSS ON OUR BACK"

Father Bill's life can be summed up in three words: faith in action. He lives out the Gospel's call to each of us to expand, to go beyond the comfortable but narrow limits we have set for ourselves, to be—like the Body and Blood of Christ—"poured out and broken for one another."

Time and again, by his actions as well as by his inspirational writings, Father Bill drives home the message that God's Kingdom can be experienced in the here and now as we become increasingly aware of God's presence in our lives and are willing to share His presence with others.

He does this with a rare blend of honesty, wit, and wisdom, leading many to regard him as a "prophet" in the truest sense of the word—not by virtue of his ability to discern the future, but by his ability to discern the truth and reveal it to others. You will be blessed as you read and respond to the many truths Father Bill reveals in this book.

The End of an Era

Inevitably the aging process catches up with each of us and in 2003, after 25 years of service, Bill decided it was time to step down as pastor of The Community of St. James.

In his usual concern for the people he was leaving behind, he had worked out a transition plan with a group of parishioners – a plan that called for a like-minded priest to succeed him and provide the parish with continuity.

In April of 2003 the Community of St. James prepared a presentation for the bishop, the personnel board and/or other representatives of the diocese. What follows is a summary of that Diocesan Presentation: "The Journey of the Community of St. James, April 2003."

Why We Are Here

- To help you further know the core of who we are, what we do, and how we try to "empty" ourselves out for others.

- To seek your blessing – Father Skeehan will eventually be retiring and we would like to discuss that with you.

Who We Are

- A community who have chosen to live in the love of Christ and "Surrender to Him in faith…"
- A community with a 38-year tradition of service:
  - Within our Parish
  - Within the larger community of Bartlesville
- A community committed to addressing issues of justice, human dignity, and peace.

State of St. James

- We serve 705 registered parishioners
  - Father Skeehan also serves St. Catherine's in Nowata.
- There is extensive lay participation at all levels.
- We are a prayerful and Sacramental community:
  - Weekly scripture study and prayer
  - Thursday morning charismatic prayer group.
  - New Testament Lenten scripture study.
  - Tuesday/Thursday Mass.
  - Eucharistic annual renewal and prayer gathering.
  - In 2002: "Year of Prayer"
  - In 2003: "Pray for Peace" – Parishioners prayed hourly every day for peace.
  - Weekly adoration before the Blessed Sacrament and weekly meditation.

- 2003 Lenten "Ashes to Easter" Renewal – weekly faith sharing groups base on Sunday Scriptures.
- More than half of our parish families are involved in community outreach programs.
- Each family financially supports an average of 5 community organizations.
- 7 organizations founded by Parishioners.
- Parish gives 30% of its income to those in need.

- **Finances**
  - Financially solvent
  - $97,000 in assets
  - $224,000 annual budget
  - No debt
  - Support DDF and Catholic Charities
  - Strong supporter of Diocese Fund for the Future; doubling our goal.

Strategic Planning for the future by parish council
Various partnerships with St. John Parish

OUTREACH ACTIVITIES FOUNDED BY ST. JAMES PARISHIONERS
- Mary Martha Outreach
- Green Country Free Clinic
- Martha's Task
- St. James' Community Assistance program

- Family Crisis and Counseling (formerly Women and Children in Crisis)
- Eldercare
- New Adolescent Parent Meal program

GROWING NEED FOR OUTREACH SERVICES IN WASHINGTON COUNTY

- Loss of Phillips Petroleum headquarters
- Extensive program cuts from reduced state funding
- Declining local sales tax collections (-6% per year)
- Bartlesville shifting demographics
- Rising unemployment
- The Washington County Unemployment Rate increased from 4.05 in January 2002 to 6% in January 2003

MARY MARTHA OUTREACH

- <u>Purpose</u>: To provide free clothing, furniture, commodity food, haircuts and household items to the needy
- For ALL God's children: no questions, no limits, no judgment.
- Founded in 1998 by St. James members
- Stipend provided by Catholic Charities
- In 4 ½ years, Mary Martha has given away:
  - 850,000 garments
  - 400 tons of food

- 3,500 pieces of furniture
- 1,500 haircuts
- 2,300 meals

VALUE $6 million (per IRS guidelines)

GREEN COUNTRY FREE CLINIC

- <u>Purpose</u>: Provide primary care and medication to those unable to afford these services.
- All physicians and assistants are volunteers.
- Clinic does not receive any funding from local, state or federal agencies.
- All donations are local

<u>St. James' Involvement</u>

- Founded by parishioners in 1988.
- Approximately 30 volunteers and 2 board members

<u>Three Programs:</u>

1. Primary Care Services
2. Patient Assistance Program
3. Mental Health and Chronic Illness

- Capable of serving 25 people a night.

"Lord, you alone can heal me, you alone can save and my praises are for you alone." Jeremiah 17:14

MARTHA'S TASK

- <u>Purpose</u>: provide training, marketing, financial support and advocacy for indigenous women.

- Encourages cottage industry and enables women to earn money.

ECONOMIC DEVELOPMENT

<u>St. James' Involvement</u>

- Founded by parishioners in 2001.

- 35 volunteers and 2 board members

- Provide majority of financial support

<u>2002 Statistics:</u>

• Served 100 women who received 924 hours of training and earned over $12,000.

"May the favor of the Lord our God be ours, Prosper the work of our hands! O' prosper the work of our hands!" Psalm 90:17

ST. JAMES COMMUNITY ASSISTANCE PROGRAM

- <u>Purpose</u>: Provide financial assistance to those in need of food, medicine, utilities, clothing and gasoline

- For <u>anyone in need</u>; not just parishioners.

St. James' Involvement
- Funding: Over $17,000 in 2002
- Operated by St. James Staff
- St. John contributes $300/month

"If you wish to be perfect, go, sell what you have and leave it to the poor, and you will have treasure in heaven. Then come follow me."   *Matthew 19:21*

Value of Services Provided – 2001
- Gasoline $6,000
- Food $9,900
- Medicine $1,800
- Utilities $6,100
- Other $2,100

ELDERCARE (LOCAL)

Purpose:
- To help seniors and caregivers navigate the issues of senior care.

Services:
- Care management, adult day care, education, trans-portation, medical equipment and caregiver support services

St. James' Involvement
- Parishioner was one of the founders
- Initially housed at St. James

St. James' Involvement

- Founded in 1983, Eldercare has grown to an umbrella group serving 1,000 people in Washington and Nowata counties.
- New 37,000 sq. ft. facility to be completed in 2004.
- Critical need for our aging community.

"Hear me, O house of Jacob, all who remain of the house of Israel, my burden since your birth whom I have carried since infancy. Even to your old age I am the same, even when your hair is gray I will bear you; it is I who have done this, I will continue, and I will carry you to safety." Isaiah 46:3-4

FAMILY CRISIS AND COUNSELING
(Formerly Women and Children in Crisis)

- Founded in 1984 as domestic violence shelter in a house on St. James property as Woman and Children in Crisis.
- Domestic abuse agency has grown to serve entire family and become a vital part of Bartlesville.

St. James' Involvement

- Parishioner was one of the founders
- Provided rent and utility-free building.
- 16 volunteers and 3 board members.
- In 2003, over 1,300 clients were served.

"Have pity on me O lord, for I am in distress: With sorrow my eye is consumed; My soul also, and my

body…I am like a dish that is broken…But my trust is in you, O lord; I say, "You are my God." Psalm 31:10-15

NEW ADOLESCENT PARENT MEAL PROGRAM
- <u>Purpose</u>: Provide a meal to adolescent mothers-to-be and young parents in the New Adolescent Parent program, which supports very young parents.
- Teaches parenting skills.
- Supports Right to Life.

<u>St. James' Involvement</u>
- Founded by parishioners in 1997.
- Parishioners provide 100% of the meals.

<u>2002 Activity:</u>
- Provided meals valued at over $9,000.
- Serve 15-25 parents a night.

CATHOLIC HOSPITALITY EXTENDED TO OTHERS
- Religious Education (K – adult)
- Parish nursing
- Senior Ministry (Luncheon/support group)
- Meeting space or building use
- Soccer fields/pavilion use
- Homebound ministry
- College students volunteer meals (Habitat for Humanity)
- On-site housing and utilities

ST. JAMES OUTREACH FUNDING

By 2002, Funding was over $100,000 per year. Over 30% of the parish budget. Almost $1 million over 25 years.

CATHOLIC HOSPITALITY (BUILDING USE) EXTENDED TO THESE SUPPORT GROUPS:

- American Cancer Society
- Cub Scouts
- Washington County 4-H Beef Club
- Mary Martha Outreach
- Eldercare
- Habitat for Humanity
- Bartlesville Genealogical Society
- Fun Addicts Clown Group
- National Alliance for the Mentally Ill
- Parkinson's Disease Support Group
- Washington County Support Group
- Depressive and Bipolar Support Group
- Girl Scouts of America
- Al-Anon
- Family Crisis and Counseling Support Groups

WE ARE SEEKING YOUR BLESSING

To continue the Journey of St. James as a Eucharistic Community striving to live the Paschal Mystery through prayer, sacrament, scripture and service, and in light of our 38 years of service to the poor we ask you:

- Appoint a pastor so that Father Skeehan, who has served the Church so well, may pursue retirement.

We know that pastoral appointments are your responsibility. To help you in the process, we believe that the personality of the new pastor should reflect the stewardship personality of St. James, so that both the priest and the parish may continue as one to live your very summons of "emptying ourselves out" in the service of others.

The chancellor, Msgr. Denis Dorney, was the lone representative of the Tulsa diocese to hear the presentation. He seemed to listen attentively and was favorably impressed by the content of the presentation. On the other hand, how the information was conveyed to "the powers that be" is not known by the parish. What the Community of St. James does know is that the Diocese of Tulsa preferred that the parish would move in a direction that had less of Vatican II's emphasis on liturgy and social justice. What transpired, thanks to the priests assigned to the Community of St. James was something of a deconstruction process of what Bill Skeehan stood for.

Evaluation of the Council Twenty Years Later – 1985

To celebrate the 20th anniversary of the completion of Vatican II, Pope John Paul II called an Extraordinary Synod of Bishops to meet in Rome from November 25 to December 8, 1985.

According to Avery Dulles, the Synod and the reports of its various discussion groups reflected two schools of thought among the bishops. The first group led by Cardinal Ratzinger (now Pope Benedict 16) and Josef Hoeffner of Germany, had, in Dulles' view, a markedly super-naturalistic point of view, tending to depict the church as an island of grace in a world given over to sin. Since "the world is falling into misery, division and violence" and since "Catholics who seek friendship with the world easily fall into materialism, consumer-ism and religious indifference…the church today must take a sharper stance against the world and seek to arouse a sense of God's holy mystery."

The second group, represented by Cardinal Hume of England and Bishop James Malone and Bernard Huberts, presidents of the USA and Canadian bishops' conferences took a "more humanistic and communi-tarian view." Dulles summarized the views of the second group:

"Convinced that great progress has been made as a result of the Council, they attributed the main difficul-ties to the failure of conservative prelates (bishops) to

carry through the reforms of Vatican II. If there is a disenchantment among youth, it is ...because the necessary reforms have been resisted and partly blocked. The Catholic Church has not yet succeeded in giving its laity an adequate sense of participation in and co-responsibility for the mission of the collegial and synodal structures so that the church may become a free and progressive society, a sign of unity in diversity, at home in every nation and every socio-logical group."

Rynne, Xavier. *John Paul's Extraordinary Synod: A Collegial Achievement* (Wilmington DEL: Michael Galzier,1986) 25, quoted in Eagan (1986) 41.

Bill Skeehan and the Community of St. James would be clearly in the camp of the second group still favoring the spirit of Vatican II and renewal. However, we must admit that the first group holding as a high value the restoration of what existed before Vatican II is gaining steam the further we get from the Council itself.

Unresolved Issues and Present Tensions

1. The practical working out of its principle of collegiality

    a At the synods of Bishops, the bishops do not decide the topics to be discussed, have a merely consultative, not legislative voice, and the final report is edited by curial officials and the pope.

b. The clergy and laity of a given diocese have no <u>official</u> voice in selecting their bishop.

c. According to the theological opinion of Cardinal Ratzinger, the bishops' conferences have no teaching authority.

d. Due in part to the lack of structures for regular and honest communication between the hierarchy and the laity, the secrecy and mishandling of criminal sexual behavior by members of the clergy have caused scandal, anger and cynicism around the globe.

2. <u>Celibacy and Catholic Priesthood</u>

a. The official church refuses to consider a change in what involves church discipline rather than doctrine.

b. Refusal to ordain women.

c. Growing number of priestless parishes.

d. Transition from sacral model of priesthood, as "dispenser of mysteries" to leadership model in forming and nurturing the faith community, especially through a ministry of word and sacrament. (These two models of priesthood are a fundamental difference between Bill Skeehan (leadership model) and Bishop Slattery (sacral model).)

3. Contraception in Marriage

John 23 had set up a commission of moral theologians, doctors, scientists, university professors, married couples, and several cardinals to discuss this issue. The commission voted overwhelmingly (64-4) to petition a change in the traditional teaching against contraception. Pope Paul 6, in office by the time the report was completed, rejected the report. In his 1968 Encyclical *On Human Life*, he upheld the minority view, which then divided Catholics and damaged the teaching authority of the papal office.

4. Conscience, Dissent, and Church Authority

Fear of dissent has caused church leaders to overstress in a defensive manner their own authority and Catholics' obligation to obedience. This tends to obscure deeper issues and reduce the credibility of the teaching office among educated Catholics.

5. The Role of Women in the Catholic Church

a. Patriarchy is expressed in the church by an exclusively male hierarchy holding all the decision-making power, by the linking of jurisdiction to ordination, and by the exclusively male language in Church documents, worship and in translations of Scripture.

b. In a 1994 Apostolic Letter, Pope John Paul II stressed that "Priestly Ordination Reserved to

Men Alone" is not only a matter of church discipline, but of doctrine concerning the nature of priesthood.

6. The Current Slow Pace of Ecumenism

There exists a discouragement, a frustration, an increasing loss of enthusiasm, even cynicism among those committed to ecumenism. This is due, for the most part, to the demands of the Congregation for the Doctrine of the Faith for almost total theological agreement in Catholic terminology with other churches.

7. Polarization and Catholic Fundamentalism

a. Intentional polarization is often more common than a willingness to work toward a common solution. Part of the polarization has come through efforts of those who desire a restoration to a pre-Vatican Council II Church.

b. A more extreme form of polarization is the contemporary phenomenon of Catholic fundamentalism. In an April 11, 1987 article in *America Magazine*, Patrick Arnold terms Catholic fundamentalism "a religious disease that focuses on nonessential matters in Catholic belief." Arnold goes on, "It stresses authority and is obsessed with questions of individual salvation and sexual morality. Official statements of the Roman magisterium are to be obeyed absolutely, but have little regard for teaching on social questions such as poverty, just wage, human rights or nuclear disarmament."

c. Catholics United for Faith (CUF) founded in 1968 to counter the dissent by Catholic moral theologians against the encyclical *On Human Life* are an example of Catholic fundamentalism. There is no such thing as "loyal dissent" allowed in the Catholic Church

We think you can surmise again how this fundamentalism would play with the opposing views of Bishop Slattery and The Community of St. James.

8. Relations with the Vatican

a. There is a growing disaffection for the Vatican on the part of large numbers of Catholics. Recent polls indicated growing disagreement between the laity and church leaders on ethical issues, especially birth control and a strong desire for more democratic procedures. Especially alienated groups are women, gay persons, divorced and remarried, single parents.

b. This disaffection obviously is not a healthy situation and is a cause of sadness for all who love the church. Yet honesty and concern for the good of the church demand that substantive issues be honestly and respectfully raised.

A Concluding Reflection

These eight areas of unresolved issues and of tensions and division in today's Catholic Church should be seen in the context of the Second Vatican Council: its emphasis on the church as all the baptized, including women, rather than the hierarchy alone; on the importance of the local church and its bishop as successor of the Apostles; on the pervasive principles of collegiality and subsidiarity that have influenced the relationship of local churches to the pope and curia. The Council's emphasis on our common baptism, on Jesus' prayer for unity so as to evangelize the world, give an urgency to Christian ecumenism. The Council's stress on religious freedom, on the primacy of one's conscience, and on the Spirit guiding individual Christians have made dissent possible and even necessary. The Council's fuller understanding of church history, of how doctrinal insights and formulations develop over time, and of the manner in which the church's magisterium operates has highlighted the important work of theologians. Thus, dissent and a certain disaffection need not mean disloyalty; rather both often proceed from a deep concern and profound love for the church. As St. Augustine reminds us: "In essentials unity, in nonessentials freedom, but in all things charity."

This last section on <u>Eight Unresolved Issues and Present Tension</u> has been taken from *Restoration and Renewal: The Church in the Third Millennium* by Joseph F. Eagan, Sheed and Ward, 1995.

First Years After Leaving St. James Parish

On Monday, May 11, 2009, Edward Jeep and Joseph Dillon were privileged to meet and interview 24 stalwart members of The Community of St. James who had thrived and grown spiritually during the ministry of Father Bill. We have used some of the material we gleaned from those interviews throughout our story. We would like to include a few more comments about what their experience was like in a parish that endeavored to live the Vatican II Renewal spirit.

<u>Comments About the Community of St. James</u>

Loretta and Van Vives – "For us it was truly a hope-filled experience. There was such an inclusive attitude with a respectful ecumenical spirit. For example, the Church building served as a tornado shelter that served the entire neighborhood. We were challenged to start the first hospice in Bartlesville and there was continually the challenge to grow spiritually. Eventually, we had a Parish Nurse who helped us develop Living Wills among other services."

Eva and Dan Boatright– "We had moved to Bartlesville from New Jersey and we were looking around to find the right church for us. One Sunday, we celebrated at St. James and our reaction was, Wow! It was so joyful, enthusiastic, welcoming and had a healing aspect to it. We knew we were <u>home</u>."

<u>Comments About Father Bill</u>

<u>Cliff Sousa</u> – "He was creative in so many ways from wood carvings out of driftwood to artistic slide presentations at special Liturgies. His homilies were filled with gospel challenges embracing social action."

"He was the conscience of the community. Whenever he was the on-call chaplain at the hospital, he could always be counted on to be there."

Several women commented on how respectful he was toward women as they served in various leadership roles including Presidents of the Parish Council.

A number of the interviewers touched on how prophetic his homilies were as he related the Scriptures to their daily life and gave us a sense of social sin.

"He was a personal friend to us as he shard meals with us. He truly enjoyed people, showed card tricks to our children and, yet he was also terrific with the elderly."

"He led by serving, a true shepherd and counselor. He learned to trust the wisdom of the group and allowed God to work in us. We became aware that he often gave away his salary to the poor, so we set up a special Skeehan Vacation bank account to which he had no access."

"He introduced us to prophetic models like Dorothy Day, Martin Luther King, Jr., Cesar Chavez, Stan Rother (Oklahoma priest who was martyred in Guatemala), etc."

"Lest we canonize Bill before his time, he had a fetish about how the chairs were lined up in a semi-circle. We finally put tape on the floor to solve the issue."

Ed Jeep and Joe Dillon would like to express their deep gratitude to Susan and Mike Murphy for hosting the day and arranging the interview. We are also very appreciative of all those who took the time to be interviewed. It was a profoundly moving experience for us to see first hand what had been accomplished by a group of people who had formed a remarkable faith community in the spirit of Jesus.

Despite the keen disappointment the parishioners experienced due to the lack of understanding shown by the diocese, nothing can take away their 26 years of lived experience of the Mystery of Christ.

"Doing the Father's work sometimes leads to conflict. Helping the poor can be seen as a threat by the rich. Telling people to love their enemies can be seen as a danger to national security. Giving food to the hungry can be seen as undercutting the economy. Performing miracles of healing through the power of God can be seen as a threat to cherished beliefs that such things just can't happen."

From *The Great Themes of Scripture,* New Testament by Richard Rohr and Joseph Martos, Saint Anthony Messenger Press, 1988. ISBN 0-86716-098-5.

AUTHORITY AND AUTHENTICITY

AUTHORITY AND AUTHENTICITY

by Edward G. Jeep

Background

Looking For Answers

An important question has haunted the generation that lived through and was formed by the Second Vatican Council: What happened to the church awakened by Vatican II? Put another way, we can ask, 'What would the church look like today if it had been faithful to the spirit and documents of the Council?' Watching the course the Catholic Church has taken during the past forty years has been painful in the extreme, especially for those of us who were most smitten by its promise. It has been like watching the slow demise of profound beauty and potentiality, given to us in our youth, seemingly too substantive to fail, yet slowly, slowly, fading into ever dimming light.

It seems to me that the answer does not lie in imitating particular post-Vatican II programs and parishes, but in discovering how such programs embodied, for those who participated in them, the vision of the Council, which was understood as a new movement of the Spirit of God, promising nothing less than new life—a new Pentecost for the Church.

So new questions emerge: How did those people become open to recasting their Catholic life into new forms? And more important: How did they become, in the process of living in the Vatican II spirit, responsive to prophetic leadership and open to personal conversion? Because those qualities were apparent during the years when the new direction was fragile, and the future of Catholic renewal uncertain.

This essay is a personal reflection on Fr. Skeehan's career, and as such is an appendix to Joe Dillon's excellent account of his pastoral achievements, "What a Vatican II Parish Looks Like." It is only comprehensible when paired with a reading of that work. I have briefly retold some of those stories, in order to put them into the context of my analysis.

This essay is also a recognition of the hundreds of men and women who were participants in the communities that formed around Bill Skeehan's ministry, and were in turn formed by the Christian life that they experienced there. In studying these questions, in preparing this book, we are not so much trying to celebrate Bill's career, though we certainly do that, but we are trying to capture for those who were not there a picture of the inner spirit shared by a whole generation of Catholics – a picture of grace offered and a promise that the Spirit would indeed "renew the face of the earth."

My presumption in writing this paper stems from my relationship with Bill Skeehan. I have known him for 49 years -- almost as long as anyone still standing. That relationship has been rich, and what follows rises out of that richness, and thus very much has written itself. My focus is Bill's authenticity, and the personal authority that stems from it. I believe that Bill's story yields enriched understanding of conversion and revelation, not just of the transcendent God, but also of what it means to be fully human. That is, in fact the central theme of the writing.

The heightened interest in this genre of personal authority has been concurrent with, and reaches a crescendo in the experience and implementation of the Second Vatican Council, which has been described by Karl Rahner as nothing less than a 're-creation of the Church.' It has been richly evidenced in the life of Bill Skeehan and many, many others: priests like Dan Berrigan and Tom Merton; laypersons such as Dorothy Day and Martin Luther King; and bishops like Oscar Romero and Cardinal Bernadine.

The authority of which I write includes within its scope the sacramental, the mystical and the prophetic. It has been especially evidenced, I believe, in its collision with the church's institutional authority, structures and practices inherited from its classical embodiment left over from the Middle Ages, and to which it is still tied.

Capturing the Story

Joe Dillon and I were fellow priests with Bill Skeehan in what, at the time, was the single Diocese of Oklahoma City and Tulsa. It was at Joe's initiative that we started this writing project. Both of us had left the priesthood but had watched Bill create two of the most vibrant parishes ever. The first was an experimental parish Bill started at the invitation of his bishop, Victor Reed, in Tulsa, Oklahoma: Resurrection Parish. The second was St. James in Bartlesville, Oklahoma. St. James had already begun its unique development under another gifted pastor, Robert Pickett. In Bill's latter appointment he had an extraordinary run of 26 years.

Joe and I had come to recognize Bill as what in sports lingo would be called a 'natural.' One day while conversing about Bill as one of the great ones, Joe turned to me and said simply, "We really have to get Bill's life on the record." Spontaneously we both knew that we just had to do that, not knowing exactly where to begin or where it would lead us. Early on Joe came up with the question that would give a focus to our efforts: What would a parish (and the church) look like if we had been decisively true to Vatican II? Perhaps the story of Bill Skeehan's pastoral experience would in some significant measure answer that question.

I went to Tulsa, sat down with Bill in his apartment, digital recorder on the table, and coaxed out his life story, which was eventually transcribed into 45 pages. It was a rich and extraordinary experience. Joe and I then spent an entire day interviewing members of St. James Parish, learning first hand their experience, understandings, and love of Bill. Joe then wrote a biographical paper, "What a Vatican II Parish and Church would look like if it had been faithful to Vatican II."

Two occurrences during and after these events stimulated my pursuit of this paper. The first was something that Bill mentioned in my interview with him: that he had always been confused by the fact that all the bishops with whom he had served seemed to have been afraid of him. From my knowledge of Bill, my immediate reply was crisp: "It does not surprise me at all. You have the deep personal authority that comes of authenticity. You can easily be threatening to bishops who tend to rely on position for their authority."

The second occurred when I happened upon the work by Karl Rahner, *Concern For The Church*, with its brilliant insight that the Council was not the result in any significant way of planning and strategy but rather was distinctively a creative act of the Spirit. A complex of factors had been arrayed by that Spirit, resulting in a change in the church's self-understanding from a

"Euro-centric" to a "world" church. This change constituted a literal re-creation, second only to the transformation initiated by Saint Paul in the first century, when the Christian community moved from its apostolic origins to its embodiment within the Greco / Roman world.

Factors thus arrayed by the Spirit had been incubating for decades and had many roots. The biblical renewal, for example, had started with the work of Pere Lagrange, OP and the Dominicans of the Pontifical Biblical Institute in Jerusalem. The liturgical renewal fostered at Benedictine monasteries like Maria Laach in Germany, and Solemnes in France, had been brought to the U.S. chiefly by Father Virgil Michel, OSB. It's insights were spread throughout the country through *Orate Fratres*, later *Worship* magazine, published at St. Johns Abbey in Collegeville, Minnesota. Those movements were part of a more general doctrinal renewal influenced by the great theological writers of the era such as Dominicans Yves Congar and Edward Schillebeeckx; Jesuits Henri De Lubac, John Courtney Murray, Piet Schoonenberg, the brothers Hugo and Karl Rahner; and diocesan priests such as Hans Kung, and many others.

What was singular about these theologians was that they spoke with an authority born of their scholarship, their pastoral experience, and their interaction within the European world that was still trying to grapple with the aftermath of the Second World War. They did not claim their institutional platforms as authority for their insights. Rather they spoke and wrote with personal authority.

What then began to pester me was the similarity between that deepening of personal authority in its sacramental, mystical and prophetic expressions, so evident in those precursors to the Council on the one hand and on the other, that same deepening of personal authority that had been so evident in Bill Skeehan's ministry, and in the ministries carried out by his parishioners.

Had they not been brought to the consciousness of their authority through similar inspirations and were they not extensions of them? If so, how had the Spirit led them to a role in furthering "its creative acts?". Finally, what if anything, did that process imply about the nature of authentic conversion?

In this regard, I believe that, after Vatican II, that same inspirations of the Spirit had called the bishops of the world to exercise that same sacramental, prophetic and mystical creativity in implementing the decisions of the Council, as had been shown by its precursors. And also that the Spirit called on the laity, in their turn, to enter into their own like authority as the People of God to answer that same call to recreation. Vatican II was in fact an invitation to the entire church to move beyond its contemporary Euro-centrism and to become a World church.

Context of the Story

The overall context of this analysis will be the hierarchical church's post Vatican II understanding of its authority and its exercise of that authority. It will focus very directly on the manner in which the post Vatican II hierarchy tended to differ from many pastors, priests and laity in the local churches in their understandings of their respective authorities as coming out of the Council.

That difference will be illustrated by two contrasting pictures:

1) The picture of the hierarchy faced with implementing the Council, sometimes using its power to control dogmatic 'purity' and at other times using it to nurture reform. How was their understanding of faith related to their understanding of dogma; and what finally was their understanding of institutional structures as 'divinely' established ?

2) In contrast to that picture is that of the local church, especially its many gifted and **prophetic** pastors, priests and laity, facing implementation of the Council as the People of God. What did that metaphor mean in their understanding of the role of the local church, and their understanding

of its own relevant authority. Did they see their task as obedience to the hierarchy as over them or as initiators of reforms with them?

I suggest that contrasts between these two pictures can reveal the extent to which the institutional church had come to the conviction that it was the locus of revelation; or even more germane to this discussion, the extent to which it had come to consciously experience itself as divine revelation rather than the medium of that revelation.

The suggestion that these possibilities are reasonable and might indeed constitute significant underlying factors in the failure of the implementation of Vatican II is not original with this writing. It is a mere echo of many others of considerably more substance: see, for example, Thomas Merton's 1966 essay, "The Other Side of Despair." Alluding to the work of Merton, George Kilcourse writes in *Aces of Freedom* (152):

(Merton) defended Karl Adam's protest against Catholic faith being presented as an intellectual assent to dogmatic propositions, nothing more. He could berate with equal force the modern Church's toying with the "mental snake-handling" that is content to establish a self-righteous oligarchy during a time of crisis and the "religious vaudeville" that trivializes religion and denigrates into salesmanship.

How anything even remotely resembling such a consciousness could have come about historically will be explored, as well as how such a consciousness has been prophetically challenged by the like of Bill Skeehan and his parishioners.

I must, before going any further, establish one very important distinction that grounds this entire discussion. It is the distinction between 'knowledge' as something acquired by the subject's intellectual acceptance of the 'truth' of doctrinal statements on the one hand, and on the other hand 'consciousness' at the level of meaning which I am suggesting can only be achieved by the subject in his or her becoming a mature, converted, and authentic human being. My point is aptly dramatized by T.S Eliot's "Four Quartets" as the plight of one who "had the experience but did not understand the meaning."

To underscore this I will briefly note humankind's historic journey to full consciousness seen as revelation. I believe that journey to be the prototype of what recurs (or of what is offered) in every human life.

Our consciousness as the human race began of course, within our unconscious oneness within creation with the Divine as its ground. From that, under the divine creative impulse, humankind was 'birthed' into its consciousness. It was this that was mythically represented in Genesis as revelation, our transformation, our rebirth from our unconscious experience to our conscious one.

We were not however by that rebirth stripped of our unconscious dimension. It continued as an important dimension of us, containing as it does, the markers of our entire unconscious experience of reality on its transcendent ground; it was and continues to be our link, as it had been in the beginning, to our sense of the whole into which we were born, including, again, its transcendent Divine ground which has always been our ground.

This becomes especially important to my further discussion of conversion, which includes the entire journey to consciousness, i.e., our birth into ego consciousness, our birth into the consciousness of our numinous center, the self, and in and through that self's experience of the resurrected Christ, birthed us in the supreme exercise of our freedom into the fullness of our humanity in Christ.

The coming of the 'Age of Enlightenment' was a 'game change.' In this 'age of reason,' the prevailing biblical understanding of the human experience of conscious- ness, with its memory and its trappings of our creation journey, was discarded as 'irrational.' It was rejected as projection, as manufactured myth, to be unmasked as subjective illusion.

The 'real' was to be understood only as that which could be directly experienced by the senses, proven, 'objectified' and demonstrated by the intellect, not as a transformation of our being as subjects by which transformation we were able to know, i.e., to come into authentic relationship with the real, with its Divine base, as we had been in the beginning.

Unfortunately, the church as if intimidated by this 'enlightenment' joined its toxic march. It took a step even farther away from its apostolic foundations. It became defensive of its core dogmas and attempted to "prove" them according to the demands of the 'age of reason.' It took the bait and began a 'me too' framing of its experience of the Divine as some THING that could be conceptually defined, objectively proven, rather than as had the apostolic church as PRESENCE with whom we come into relationship by a transformation of our very beings as co-natural sons and daughters of the Triune God, as other Christs.

Of this tendency, the church's issuance and reliance on the Baltimore Catechism seems to witness, as does much of our scholastic philosophical / theological heritage.

The discussion of consciousness, though it provides the context of this story, is presented only in its very broadest connotations. But I suggest it can be seen as exquisitely germane as that context into which Vatican

II came to clarify this muddle, i.e., the difference on the one hand between God as object grasped by the intellect, and on the other hand, the God of mystery grasped by the wholeness of the subject by its transformed consciousness. Or to put it more simply: to assert the difference between an 'objective' intellectual grasp of the existence of God, by which we act 'as if' there is a God, as compared to the experience of God in which we can act 'with' God.

To this end, I will highlight the insight of Bernard Lonergan into what constitute the 'imperatives' to getting to the level of meaning, taken from Bernard Lonergan's work of the same title: *INSIGHT*. Those imperatives as understood by him constitute the universal 'method' of achieving understanding of our human experience at the level of meaning, i.e., penetrations into the fundamental calculus of relating to that meaning, and as its base, the Divine.

And finally it is my view, that the two most pivotal insights into human consciousness of modern times are summarized by Bernard Lonergan as the "self transforming subject," and by Carl Jung as the "individuating self," both of which, I contend, have brought the notion and the experience of conversion as consciousness, miles ahead of its classical meaning.

Contrasting Pictures of Implementation

THE HIERARCHY'S PERFORMANCE POST VATICAN II

It is widely recognized that the church, following its first "re-creation," from an apostolic church into a Greco-Roman or classical existence, inherited several major vulnerabilities. In the first place, there has been a deep investment in the 'changelessness' of revelation as something objective, already defined thus determined and understood. That determination and that understanding was derived from a classically established metaphysics that was seen as the guide to understanding the meaning of experience, rather than a metaphysics that was derived from that experience.

Regarding comprehension it was understood that if God cannot mislead, then all that is thus understood as divinely revealed must be adequate to the Known, rather than limited or provisional in keeping with the limitations of the knower.

In a similar way, the Catholic Church has established a concept of perfection that is applied to its hierarchical structures, based on a belief in the divine origins of those structures. It is a perfection that is believed to exist despite the limitations or even corruption of the holders of office within that hierarchy. This has resulted in a form of control based on divine selection, with little need of, provision for or exposure to requirements of accountability. Indeed, any challenge to the actions or structures of the hierarchy were considered to be challenges to God's own perfection. It is not surprising that the typical reaction to the 'turn to experience' and the 'turn to the subject' has been resistance, denial, and cries of heresy from bishops and cardinals.

Describing the impact of that denial, and the prophetic challenge to it by the ministry of Bill Skeehan and many others of his kind, is the rest of our story.

Let us look now, in some detail at the history involved. Pope John XXIII, who had called the Council, apparently out of the blue, gave every appearance of being a converted and mature Christian, living from his spiritual center, his numinous self. From all appearances he acted as an authentic subject in calling for the opening of the windows of the church. In this he exercised not just his authority as pope, but his personal authority as a converted and authentic Christian subject.

The suddenness of the pope's announcement, and the freedom with which he exercised his authority in calling for a council went against the grain of the rigid hierarchical culture that dominated the church at that time. It threw much of the hierarchy, especially members of the Curia, into deep suspicion and confusion.

Many cardinals and bishops had been promoted to their positions largely because of their faithfulness to the themes of classical thought. They had not experienced nor had they been open to vigorous questioning of their institutional authority. Little attention had been called to the possibility of personal bias, or of the way they privileged the claims of nationality, of maleness, or of European, Caucasian culture. There was little provision for being held accountable within the community by each other, and especially not by the laity. They were therefore cut off from the increasingly demanding questions of modernity, and were thus deprived of one of the most basic opportunities for conversion. They had been isolated from much of the modern culture's progressive development, and especially the challenge of its developing personal authority, to balance that of their hierarchical authority.

Encouraged by Pope John, and assisted by the Council periti, among whom were those same men who had made up the complex movement of the Spirit that had lead to the Council, the Council committees did produce a critical mass of proposals for reform that were discussed, amended, finally approved by the Council and signed by the Pope. To some extent it seemed later to have happened without the full comprehension of the bishops. Many of them, as was witnessed in the post Council positions they took, did not seem to grasp the import of the documents they had passed, taken as a whole.

With the untimely death of John XXIII on June 3, 1963, implementation of the Council was left to his successor, Pope Paul VI, a classically trained prelate. He died in 1978, after a reign of only 15 years. He was followed by Pope John Paul I, who died after only 30 days in office, having had little impact on the affairs of the church. It was not until the reign of his successor, Pope John Paul II whose long reign extended from 1978 to 2005, that the voices of reaction began to be heard in earnest, and decisions were made that began to turn back the clock.

Pope John Paul II was an extraordinary personage in many ways, a tragic one in others. The horizon of his reign seemed to many of us to have been dominated by a dramatic flair not uniquely attuned to ego transcendence. He seemed not to have been alert to distortions that might derive from the 'rock star' status he achieved through his world tours, or from his early years of ministry in a communist dictatorship. In any case, it seems that he held a strong bias against the questioning of church beliefs and policies voiced by laity, lower clergy and theologians, and a strong bias towards the imposition of central control. This combination effectively reversed the momentum created by the documents and directions supported by John XXIII and Vatican II.

Over the course of his 27-year reign, he made episcopal appointments seemingly based on loyalty to his vision of an orderly and orthodox Church. Because of his long reign, more than 80% of the bishops ministering today were his appointees.

LOSING SIGHT OF THE PROMISE

It was thus that in the post-Vatican II years church leadership gradually became distracted from implementing the Council mandates. The hierarchy seemed especially inattentive to the Bill Skeehans of the world who were operating at the local level where great achievements at renewal were being made. Leadership seemed reluctant to take local realities seriously, and in some cases seemed to reject what they saw, even developing a growing attitude of irritation at what seemed to constitute a challenge to their own authority.

What was the meaning of the refusal of church leaders to recognize where and how a re-creation of the church was happening on the local level? Was it a conscious de facto decision against renewal? Unquestionably an intense conflict had developed between the bishops and pastors who went forward with personal authority to implement the theological insights and practical decrees of Vatican II, and those bishops and priests who resisted such change.

Questions were soon raised concerning the authenticity of hierarchical authority, leading to a crisis in the credibility and quality of its leadership. A growing gap between the prophetic voices awakened by the Spirit during the period on the one hand, and on the other hand the appointed and anointed institutional authorities who seemed increasingly dedicated to a false notion of changelessness.

My interpretation of this movement in the post-Vatican church was reinforced by Michael McCarthy, Professor Emeritus of Theology at Vassar College, Poughkeepsie, N.Y., and a prominent student of Bernard Lonergan's thought on human consciousness:

The new consciousness that it (Vatican II) called for included "a shift from the cultural classicism of the Middle Ages" understanding of the permanence and irreversibility of inherited institutions and practices, to a historically minded culture which is critically dynamic, with an understanding that there is need to combine change and constancy, tradition and innovation, continuity and systemic reform in the World Church *("The loss of Effective Authority: A Crisis of Trust and Credibility*," unpublished speech, 2005).

The shift of which Michael McCarthy speaks is at the core of our discussion: it was a shift of viewpoint, from the static one of classicism to the dynamic one of historicity. His is not the only testimony to that of course. Bernard Lonergan wrote:

The basic issue is between a static and a dynamic viewpoint. If the viewpoint is static, then from the very start everything is settled. Nothing new can be added at any point after one has started. On the other hand, if the viewpoint is dynamic, then there can be added any number of reflections and discoveries that at the start were not included in one's assumptions. ("The Ongoing Genesis of Methods," The Lonergan Review, vol. I, n1, 30)

With modernity, indeed had come a very large number of 'reflections and discoveries,' and the 'viewpoint' had very much changed. The world had come upon stunning new 'discoveries,' such as the evolution of all living things, the expanding cosmos, and the re-imagining of materiality proposed by quantum physics. Alongside of this, depth psychology had developed new insights into the very way individuals come to know the 'real' and are present to it and how an individual's consciousness emerges from the unconscious and the ego, into its numinous and finally its divinized self.

In this latter activity of knowing and presence, the subject's attention shifts from 'taking a good look' at something that is already out there, to entering into relationships with the 'real' by becoming itself real, authentic. It is no longer possible for the thoughtful person to see the world as static, something already out there. Meaning and understanding have become somewhat like 'catching a fish in a flowing stream.' The recognition of this changed perception has been gradual, it was developmental, and within the 'psyche' of its development it contains what might be called its own genetic code, just as our bodies carry the DNA that identifies and shapes the physiology of human development.

Finally, regarding the way this viewpoint has reshaped our theological understandings, Richard Rohr writes that "faith is more how to believe than what to believe" (*The Naked Now*, 2009, 116); and Rohr quotes Lonergan, "conversion is the experience by which one becomes an authentic human being" (89).

For the purposes of this paper, as I have stated earlier, the trailblazers of this consciousness transforming genetic study are the depth psychologist Karl Jung, and the cognitional theorist Bernard Lonergan.

The documents of Vatican II spoke to the church from a changed, historical-developmental understanding of its own reality. It announced that in viewing the world, one needed to recognize, that everything had not been settled; a great number of "reflections and discoveries" about the church's understanding of what it means to be human, and what it means to be Christian, and what conversion is all about had not been included among its classical assumptions, and now they needed to be added. Vatican II was, for the Catholic Church, a way to play 'catch up.' Most Western thinkers had made a shift from the classical viewpoint many years before, and its implications were evidenced in secular culture.

Unfortunately, the church already had a history of rejecting it.

A CHANGE OF CONSCIOUSNESS

The cultural transition from a static to a dynamic consciousness has been described by philosophers as a 'turn to the subject.' The 'turn' as it has now come to be understood was a shift from 'objectivity' as the touchstone of truth, to 'authentic subjectivity' as the touchstone of truth. This has constituted an important watershed entailing nothing less than a shift in the understanding of understanding, that is, of how we come to know. A full study of the insights that occasioned that shift lies beyond the scope of this writing. To approach it by over-simplification would be risky, and would fail to do it justice.

However, as I have noted, I believe that the shift, in its broadest perspective, constitutes an expansion of human consciousness, and further, I believe that the resulting consciousness is 'sacramental' i.e., an experience of the Transcendent as physically and spiritually present. Most important, I see it as a guided, yet intentional process, inherent within the human psyche, drawing us to fullness. Further, I believe that the insights of Bernard Lonergan and Carl Jung are a guide to help us recognize the profound implications of the grasp of grace, i.e., the Divine in the ordinary, made possible through the new consciousness. The change is reshaping the consciousness of individual Christians, of the People of God and of the institutional church; a consciousness of what it means to be fully human in and through Christ; a consciousness that is sacramental at its deepest level.

The DNA-like 'in-scriptions' which are seen in Lonergan's transcendental method, and in Jung's discovery of human development as a journey from ego to self, i.e., the person's growing consciousness of and commitment to his or her spiritual or numinous center. The end result of such development, I understand as essentially a coming to see the self and world as sacramental. As Bernard Lonergan has written,

For it is now apparent that in the world mediated by meaning, and motivated by value, objectivity is simply the consequence of authentic subjectivity, of genuine attention, genuine intelligence, genuine reasonableness, and genuine responsibility. (1972, Method in Theology, 265)

Lonergan therefore identifies the turn to the subject as a shift from classical thought in which the object's intelligibility was seen as controlling, to the subject's internal operations as controlling the process of coming to know. The accuracy of our knowledge will depend on the authenticity of our subjectivity. What Lonergan is telling us then, is that in order to come to know the real we must in the process become real ourselves.

Becoming real, authentic, fully conscious, for Lonergan is only achieved through what he calls the "Transcendental Method." This is accomplished by undertaking the transcendental operations that he cites, by which the ego and its biases and projections are transcended, and the subject achieves in authenticity a genuine relationship with the true at the level of meaning. Those genuine operations, each of which represents progressive "horizons" of consciousness are: being attentive, being intelligent, being reasonable, being responsible, and being in love. Movement from, to, and through each of these operations constitute experiences of conversion toward one's 'numinous' center.

Thus Lonergan moves the understanding of Christian conversion light years beyond that of classical thought.

The psychologist Carl Jung, in his turn, describes the subject's creative encounter with the unconscious in his notion of individuation. For him, individuation is the process which draws the psyche to greater discernment, to greater clarity; and makes conscious the treasures of the unconscious. It is the experience of the archetypal riches of that unconscious. They (archetypes) bear the promise to the psyche for a positive interaction with them, their promising depth to human life, its potential for authentic relationship with the cosmos, and the human family, great riches of talent, wholeness, and fulfillment, all intimations of the Divine ground.

"I have come that you might have life and have it to the full."

On the negative side, individuation is the process of confrontation by the human psyche with its negative complexes and archetypes, ego demands with its myriad complexes and projections. To Jung, if the individual does not bring such distorting complexes to consciousness, (which the psyche is always promoting) he or she will be ruled by them, fixated within a false self.

Thomas Merton saw individuation, as the movement from the false self to the true self.

For our understandings here, and that of Lonergan, success in that journey can only be understood as an encounter with our Divine Ground, incarnation, conversion, and above all, an exercise of our gift of freedom, perfecting it in an intentionally chosen course to which our Divine Ground guides us. Therefore this movement toward the individuated self is in real measure a contemplative as well as a rational pursuit.

In more common language, this change in consciousness of which I speak, the turn to the subject, can be described as a shift from classical philosophy's treatment of knowing as a spectator sport, as taking a look at something that is already 'out there,' prepackaged unchanging truths. Since the turn to the subject, knowing is understood as a participation sport.

I believe that this is the crux of it. In the participation sport' of learning, the subject does not stay on the side lines looking to others, authorities, to establish certainty of the true. The subject must get into the game; he or she is not just an observer, but the key player in the 'game' of learning. His or her entire learning enterprise is based on the subject's own experience, not someone else's. It is a reflection on that experience, moving through rigorous questioning from horizon to horizon of meaning, and finally arriving at its authentic meaning, truth and value.

What does that mean to us? Nothing, unless we experience it. Only if we 'appropriate' both the process and the insights that it yields, not just the ideas that describe the reality, but our own self both in our encounter with its reality as well as in our action of coming to know in the exercise of it, only then can we approach authenticity. And, the only thing that is unchanging in its makeup is the method, not previously determined meanings.

Lonergan is clear that the movement through each of the operations of knowing makes deep demands. He sees that in our compulsion to achieve certainty, we can too easily settle for lower horizons of consciousness, i.e., for stubbornly held 'opinions.' The contrary passion for truth demands that we hold off 'closure' until we have exhausted all the 'hanging' questions. Within this method it is precisely these hanging questions that can propel us progressively through the developmental horizons of consciousness; only by the conversions that they invite us to, can we hope to approach the horizon of the transcendent God. Only thus can we avoid clutching the security blanket of our bias and the comfort of ideology, and the defense of our flawed ego.

Implementation Based On Prophetic Authority

What follows is my own version of a Lonergarian and Jungian analysis of the "journey to conversion/authenticity" experienced by Bill Skeehan and by the communities he served. One personal note before tracing those journeys: for the most part I was not directly a party to them. The events took place in the Tulsa or eastern half of the diocese, where Bill had become a pastor. While I remained stationed in the Oklahoma City or western half of the diocese. And also, much of the story took place after I had left the priesthood in 1969. Nonetheless, I remained personally close to Bill and his activities throughout.

JOURNEY FROM EGO TO SELF

Bill, youngest of five children, developed a special bond with his older sister Pat, a bond he retained throughout his adult life. Early he realized he was a natural leader as was his sister Pat, he the president of his high school class, the president of his college fraternity and later its national president. His sister was the president of her sorority. He was a popular young man with many talents: commercial artist, social skills, exceedingly good at public speaking. It was his skill in public speaking that broke him out of the pack. While employed as a graphic artist for the National Office of the Junior Chamber of Commerce, he came to the attention of the leadership because of his gifts as a skilled communicator. Within months he was elevated to the position of director of its membership division. At that time he was in clover, his prospects seemed unlimited, and it became easy for him to revel in it.

In the midst of his ego ride Bill was knocked off that horse. One evening, at a Notre Dame Club party with his cousin-in-law Katie Deck Skeehan, Bill in engaging in what he thought of as spirited social bantering, apparently had some sharp edges, because Katie suddenly turned to him and said with absolute aplomb, "You are one of the most self centered persons I have ever known."

Bill was stunned. Absolutely speechless. So much so that he withdrew from the party, went home and brooded for hours. Katie had hit a nerve, and the more he thought about what she said, and the high respect he had for her, the more a light began to go on. Deep in his psyche he began to realize that she was right! Later he called her on the phone to tell her so, and thanked her for what she had said.

This was a life changing experience, a great gift. It was the beginning of the transcending process which Jung called "individuation"; a conversion from his ego centeredness to his deeper self. That process continued, and eventually led to a decision to enter the seminary.

JOURNEY TO COMMUNITY CONSCIOUSNESS

In the fall of 1954, after having earned his degree from Tulsa University in commercial art, and having worked four years for the Junior Chamber of Commerce, Bill entered Saint Thomas Seminary. As it happened I entered with him. From the beginning Bill had about him the aura of 'personhood.' He was a calm person with no sharp edges, more of a presence than any hint of self assertiveness. Discussions developed with and around him. He was very much his own man.

Because he was 'older'(a 'delayed vocation' in the parlance of the time) seminary officials determined that he should take two extra years of college, because, they explained, he had not taken college level courses in scholastic philosophy. Bill took the setback calmly, as it was becoming increasingly clear to him that the seminary was something to be endured, rather than to be enrichment.

After ordination and as a pastor of the experimental parish, Resurrection, Bill established what the hallmark of his priesthood became: after prayer, a study of church documents and theological works, he acted on his own authority. An understanding of the church as community became the underpinning of his ministry, informing all of his thinking. Circular seating plans were used for every interaction, whether casual or formal, every Parish Council meeting, teaching/learning situation, even liturgical celebrations. This was done not only to make possible genuine interaction, but to lead the participants to experience themselves and to operate as a community where in the presence of the Spirit, they could truly deal with one another face to face, equal and free.

"Christianity is community" was his mantra.

JOURNEY INTO POVERTY CONSCIOUSNESS

This journey started in his family affluence of Los Angeles and progressed to the poverty of North Tulsa. His mentor and Christic partner for that journey was Dan Allen. Dan came from a family of eight siblings who struggled through the depression in the throes of poverty. Dan's relationship with Bill stemmed originally from their association as fellow assistant pastors at Sacred Heart Parish in Okalahoma City under one of Okalahoma's great pastors, Msgr. Lueke. During that period they collaborated on developing programs and materials to train lay volunteers who were flocking to Oklahoma on the winds of Vatican II. The focus was on building the kingdom of God, in justice, for which Dan was the masterful guide.

Later, Dan having left the priesthood, their relationship centered on Dan's work in starting one of the most unique social support organizations ever, Neighbor for Neighbor. The people Dan gathered including volunteers, donors, people in need, people on their feet who returned to help others, constituted a community of the poor, where being a neighbor meant being responsible for that neighbor, where being helped meant becoming a helper. Under Dan's creative leadership and later ably assisted by Bill, it achieved significant recognition by and impact on the larger community of Tulsa. Literally thousands of volunteers, both the poor and the well-off, became through their connection to NfN, true neighbors not just by proximity but by mutual respect and support. Their years of shared effort in this enterprise wedded the volunteers to the poor not as benefactor but as brothers and sisters.

The friendship between Dan and Bill was epitomized by their Monday sojourns at their "Golf Pub," the river retreat built by Dan, to which Bill and Dan and the third member of their triumvirate, Bob Pickett (who replaced Bill at Resurrection when Bill moved to St. James in Bartlesville) repaired weekly to size up the world and their addressing of it. It was probably those days in mutual banter that cemented their deep commitment to Dame Poverty.

Dan had not learned 'about' poverty in his childhood. He had 'become' poverty. What he had become was free; free of possessions. And as such he too had moved into his own authority. He experienced poverty as a value, and had made a clear judgment. He embraced it. He would live as a poor man.

For both Dan and Bill the state of poverty that they embraced and saw in others was not romanticized. They knew that it could be and often was brutish and overwhelming, that it often led to self pity, but not always, and not necessarily. What was essential for them was what could be met in poverty. What they saw and experienced and found redemptive of both the poor and the wealthy, was that in coping with de facto poverty something very surprising can be discovered about human freedom which is the pearl of great price, so perfectly described by Thomas Merton as meeting up with your true self.

Just how Bill was tutored by Dan to come himself to live as a poor man, is buried in the rich complexities of their life-long friendship. But what can be examined is how Bill lived as a poor man. He gave away most of whatever he took in and his parishes were nurtured by him, to a similar freedom, in their sharing with poor neighbors. In fact, the monies donated to Neighbor for Neighbor by Bill's two parishes, over the years that Bill served as pastor, exceeded one million dollars.

JOURNEY TO SHARED POWER

The journey from power 'over' to power 'with' moves us explicitly to conversion on the institutional level. It implies not only a journey from power 'over' to power 'with,' but invariably causes a pushback from the reluctant 'losers' of power.

This journey begins, as we have seen in Joe Dillon's essay, " What a Vatican II Parish Looks Like," begins in the context of the Diocesan Pastoral Board. Its monthly meeting scheduled for Feb.17, 1971 proved to be fateful. Joe Dillon had been recently elected to the board as the priests' representative. Before he left for the meeting, he was called by Dan Allen and Bill Skeehan who asked to see him prior to the meeting. It happened that W. K. Warren, founder and owner of the Warren Oil Company, had written the bishop with an offer to donate a debt-free cathedral and chancery to the Tulsa Diocese, which was soon to be established. Mr. Warren had already funded a magnificent Catholic hospital, St. Francis Medical Center, close to where the cathedral was proposed to be built. Both properties happened to be in the boundaries of Resurrection Parish. There was an odd stipulation to the offer: Bill Skeehan would have to be removed as pastor.

Bill did not understand the connection between such a gift and the appointment of a pastor. There was no theological or indeed any reasonable basis for it. What right did a wealthy donor have to make priestly appointments? Bill felt he had to take a stand. Such an arbitrary interruption of leadership in any parish would be harmful to it, particularly one that had no reference to the good of the parish or its people. It seemed to Bill that it constituted an irresponsible exercise of the power of wealth over a parish and a diocese, which if the bishop concurred, would be an equally irresponsible exercise of power by the bishop over his parish and its parishioners.

At the meeting Joe Dillon took on the board, opening a huge controversy. The bishop was taken aback by the unexpected prospect of his priests opposing the gift. Because Bill believed only in power exercised with the people, he knew that it was not up to him to make the case against this offer. The community had to determine, with him, what it should do in the face of this apparent abuse of power. The parish did in fact decide to act. It called for a meeting with the bishop. The meeting was convened in a large arena, and there was standing room only. Virtually the entire parish community turned out, not all of one accord. Many from outside the parish were in attendance as well, priests, concerned laity, and some members of the press. There were strong sentiments on both sides of the issue.

The bishop presented his case, and was politely received. The chair of the parish council responded.

He was measured. He spoke of the imbalance of a huge largesse within an affluent area of a diocese when there were large pockets of poverty which cried out for compassion. He raised the ethical question of a wealthy donor stipulating an unrelated condition: the removal of the community's pastor, with potential harm to the community's well being. There were responses, and counter responses.

Bill also took the floor, and spoke of the demand of his conscience to oppose the bishop in this matter for the sake of his community, and proposed as a condition of the gift that an equal amount of money be given to alleviate the plight of the poor. The meeting moved to a tense climax. A straw vote was recommended, and taken. The opposition to the gift was overwhelmingly in the ascendant. There was a standing ovation. A few days after the meeting the donor withdrew his offer. In retrospect regarding W. K Warren's move to oust Bill Skeehan as pastor of Resurrection Parish, it seemed that Bill's editorializing in the Tulsa World newspaper about the excesses caused by market mechanisms' impact on the poor at least partially explained his coolness towards him.

This was a conversion experience for Resurrection Parish. The parish as a whole had experienced the controversy. It had made a collective analysis of the issues involved in the acceptance or rejection of the offer. The parish had made a collective decision to act on its own authority, had demanded consultation, and in the consultation had persuasively pressed its case. The community had undergone a dramatic, intellectual, moral, and religious conversion. And they prevailed on their own, not delegated authority. This is authentic conversion.

JOURNEY TO SACRAMENTAL CONSCIOUSNESS

Bill's remarks for the 20th Anniversary of 'Neighbor for Neighbor' set this journey out beautifully.

In the Gospel of St. John we read:

> *The Word became flesh: he came to dwell*
> *Among us; through him all things came*
> *To be; no single thing was created without*
> *Him. All that came to be was alive with*
> *Life and that life was the light to humankind.*
> *The light shines on in the dark and all the*
> *Darkness has not quenched it.*

We have of course, ever since then, made frantic and deliberate efforts to change flesh back into words. Words, words, words. Words from scholars-words-words from politicians-words from preachers, words, words, words. We have through a blizzard of words, denied the incarnation. "The word became flesh"…The Word did not become word-the word became flesh… the word came to dwell among us-to live-to abide-to fully enter the human condition…and since that Final Word of God is risen and lives, then that Word still becomes flesh, still abides in us. But unfortunately we have reduced the Word to words. We have taken his flesh from him………and dry bones remain." (Unpublished paper)

Whenever Bill found himself caught up in a theological conversation he would invariably climb his way out by a protestation that he was not a theologian, that he was a homilist. And homilist he was, among the very best. His homilies came as close as any use of words can, to becoming flesh, in sacrament.

That is demonstrated in these words of Bill from another of his homilies:

We cannot give thanks for wealth unless it is shared.

We cannot give thanks for talent unless it is used for others.

We cannot give thanks for clout, unless it liberates those without clout.

We cannot give thanks for our house or home, unless we welcome the stranger." (Unpublished)

Each line describes a movement of conversion: from value to responsibility for change, from word to flesh.

But those were only small steps on his journey to the 'Flesh' of Christ.

His understandings of sacrament were larger; he saw everything as sacrament! Everything, that is, that is real: real bread, not for example, bread that is denatured into something that that does not resemble it. Why would anyone employ a symbol by denaturing it, which is to de-flesh it?

Real meals for real hunger. Real weddings not productions; real celebrations of committed love, joy not gaiety. Everything in authentic community because Christianity is community.

Real also were the many evenings around the tables in the homes of his parishioners, continuing Eucharist, as Eucharistic perhaps as any other Eucharist. Both were real to him.

Bill's best use of words was to use them against themselves; pointing unstintingly to presence, the en-fleshed and en-fleshing Christ.

JOURNEY TO JUSTICE CONSCIOUSNESS

We have said of Bill that he was a 'natural' He came at things not through the abstractions of concepts, and least of all from ideology. He had followed the gracious but unending path of conversion. In it, that complex of conversions, psychic, intellectual, moral and religious as identified by scholars, were conflated by him into one loving sweep. He saw things as a whole not as a collection of pieces. And indeed his manner of experiencing them was itself holistic. For him the human desire to know, as meaning, and as value, included an unquestioned responsibility to act to bring them to life. Comprehension was not complete until he took responsibility to bring justice to those without justice, power to those without power. They were all of one cloth, and it all came out of Presence, and was evidenced by Presence.

His homilies were unstinting calls for that justice. The Community of St. James served an area in which the well educated and affluent had gathered. His homilies elucidated clearly to those professionals and lawyers and corporate heads what the end game of the economy was: not the profit of shareholders, not the compensation of corporate CEO's, not the aggrandizement of political leaders, the end game was the common good, the economy was for the whole, not selectively for its parts; surely all of these leaders and authority figures were important to it, but theirs was in the end an instrumental role; it was by them but in the end not for them. The economy was a great deal larger than them. And as he looked out at them from his place it the circle, with his level gaze, they knew that they had met their match.

And there is ample evidence that the levelness of that gaze became their own as they saw with new eyes the poor and especially the structures that they had condoned that kept them in that condition.

JOURNEY TO CALVARY CONSCIOUSNESS

For Bill, retirement was his Calvary. After 26 fruitful years as pastor of the Community of Saint James, Bill's health was slowing him down, and he decided that it was time to resign. The Community had hoped it would never happen, and when it did their sorrow was deep. In his leaving they were determined to communicate the love the Community had for him, and the communal love amongst themselves for their world and for the poor that they had come to experience with him. Equal to that was their determination that it would continue. And their determination necessitated that the community participate in the selection of his successor as pastor.

The Parish Council acted decisively. It arranged an early meeting with the chancellor of the diocese, Msgr. Dennis Dorney, and then set about crafting a presentation clearly spelling out all the aspects of the Community's present status: the rich Christian values they had come to understand and grow into, how they had collectively decided to act on those values, and what they had in like manner accomplished in doing so. It was a primer of what a Vatican II parish should and could be. It was brilliant. In the interest of preserving and continuing in that same vein as a community it requested that it take an active role in the selection of their next pastor.

When the meeting with the chancellor was held, the presentation was flawless. He listened. There was little discussion. What followed was entirely unexpected. A few weeks later the request was summarily denied.

What then ensued was the aftermath of Vatican II revisited, its failures dramatically replayed, its embodied mystery in skyrocket display.

Hard upon that showdown, the selection of the next pastor was made. The priest that was selected, to the astonishment of everyone, especially Bill, had nothing in his background or in his makeup that bore any positive relationship with the accomplishments of the community, the depth of its community life, the vitality of its outreach to its larger community, its sensitivity to sacrament as Presence, none of it.

Worse, when the new pastor was installed, he undertook unmistakable efforts to dismantle all of its richness, piece by piece. Gone were the circles, gone was the justice outreach, and gone was the movement toward authentic Christian conversion that had been the course of that community under Bill's leadership. Without any of the scholarly theological language breaking it down to its psychic, intellectual, moral, and religious components, the community had moved through them under the tutelage the 'natural' Bill Skeehan. It had moved as individuals and as community towards their spiritual center, their numinous selves. The people of St. James had transcended much of the baggage of the Church of Classicism, especially its rigid hierarchical structures, and had come to an understanding of itself as the people of God, the Church. But the bishop's appointment of a pastor had turned all of the engines of that dynamism around into a demolition derby. And by way of any explanation, all that drifted back to the community were the reported comments of the bishop, that Father Skeehan had been too much of a social action priest.

As I have noted earlier, Bill found that bishops seemed to be afraid of him. There was now indeed ample evidence that they had. Surely that was in play when the bishop allowed Bill to remain as pastor for 26 years. Could fear also have been in play in replacing Bill with the pastor that he did? Was it a way to take control of the parish with a vengeance after Bill no longer had any institutional authority, as compensation for having so long been afraid to control it? It is not too hard to guess what was mostly in play here: asserting control, demonstrating who was in charge. Could it have been any farther from the pastoral approach of Bill Skeehan?

Such an appointment is surely not unrelated to the mystery of the failure of implementation following

Vatican II, and to the crisis of leadership that has been alluded to here. In short it might be understood as a picture of a raw collision of an unconverted leadership with a converted people.

And that in fact, is the conclusion of this writing. What was displayed in the hierarchy's tendency towards negative reactions to pioneering local initiatives, was what was at the heart of the crisis obstructing the implementation of Vatican II, that is, the gap that has developed between appointed leadership and personal authenticity. That gap has erupted into tension between hierarchical authorities and local pastors and laity who have come into their own authenticity and personal authority. The hierarchical end game is to obstruct and control the creativity and freedom of the exercise of that authority. In their defense, they simply do not understand it. They had come to live in different worlds, with very dissimilar horizons: one in a church frozen in rigid controlling structures and meanings, the other in an historic church in which the very meaning of conversion has changed.

To say that the bishop's pastoral appointment and his destructive actions were a source of pain and suffering for Bill would be an understatement of major proportions. They were for him his Calvary. He simply could not comprehend them. His strongest, but not his deepest, first reaction was in the assertion that the Bishop had destroyed 26 years of his life. He went into a depression that was prolonged, with in-effective measures of relief. It was his fateful cry of Calvary: *"My God, my God, why have you forsaken me!"* It was seen by those who were with him in it as his dark night.

That it was in fact a continuation of his conversion experience now seems clear. He had been set on that journey so many years before when he was up-ended by his cousin-in-law's deflation of his ego, and through it liberating him for a life long journey of conversion, for a merging of his life with the God of Jesus.

Much of his pain was not pain for himself, but for his beloved community. Later interactions with his community and its membership have brought healing. He has come to see that what was been accomplished, has been in fact a conversion of real substance, a change of consciousness that simply will not die. It was an experience of that mystery of the profound relationship among subjectivity, objectivity and being, all of which are gathered together as one in a participation in the consciousness of God. How and in what form it will live on is a matter for hope and faith, but that hope and that faith live on in that community, and in Bill.

The light had shone in their darkness, and the darkness had not overcome it.

One final word regarding Fr. Bill Skeehan's role in all of this. Although his importance has been reiterated often, it has not and cannot be fully comprehended. His own deep humility obscures it. One thing at least is clear. What he accomplished, and who he is, is a work of art. He saw, as do we, that what happened in and through him was the work of the Spirit. It is also my conviction, as I intimated at the beginning of this writing, that Bill's whole life has been put together by that Spirit in much the same manner as was the Council that enlivened him. It is also my conviction that he provided prophetic leadership in pointing to where the Church not only can go, but will go. Who he is, and what he was able to accomplish in those parishes and those parishioners that he served, have become a beacon to that possibility, and those communities are now archetypal of what is to come.

The Now

If we continue in the church we will all of necessity be continuing in the mystery of our baptisms: a re-creation of ourselves into Christ. And this, I suggest, must be part and parcel of our collective re-creation of the church into a world church, because it is only at the end of that journey of re-creation, beyond all bias and projection and into authenticity that we will arrive at our cosmic selves, centered as we will be, in a numinous universe by and in a truly world church.

How comprehensible is that? Perhaps a 'turn' to the poetry of T. S. Eliot can be helpful. In the conclusion of 'Four Quartets' he describes where we will be at the end of all of our explorations of meaning. At that time we will:

- Arrive where we started,

- And know the place for the first time;

- A condition of complete simplicity

- Costing not less than everything.

- (The Complete Poems and Plays, 1971)

Appendix

Let me add this final word regarding the emphasis I have placed on the works of Lonergan and Jung as spokespersons for the turn to authenticity, its importance to 'objectivity,' and to a fuller notion of Christian conversion. Lonergan and Jung point to the coincidence in knowing of judgment and responsibility, and the way the process opens us up not just to knowledge but to truth, and to being. I believe that their insights point beyond the merely rational, to the mystical. I am reminded of Karl Rahner's assertion that, "in the future Christians will either be mystics or there will be no Christians."

The two thinkers might be seen as representatives of an abstract understanding, that is, as an intrusion in this study of the practicalities of two specific parishes and their pastor. Both men's contributions were indeed, principally in the realm of theory. As Lonergan has repeatedly argued: dismissal of well founded theory is the surest way to impracticality.

For further reading on these subjects, I recommend:

Haughey, John C., SJ. *Where Is Knowing Going?: The Horizons of the Knowing Subject.* Washington, DC: Georgetown University Press, 2009.

Johnson, Elizabeth A., CSJ. *Quest for the Living God:Mapping Frontiers in the Theology of God.* NY: Continuum International Publishing Group, 2007.

Rohr, Richard, OFM. *The Naked Now: Learning To See As the Mystics See.* NY: Crossroads, 2009.

Dourley, John P *On Behalf of the Mystical Fool: Jung on the Religious Situation*, NY: Routledge, 2010.

Kilcourse, George. *Ace of Freedom: Thomas Merton's Christ*, IN, University of Notre Dame Press, 1966.

Edward Jeep

May, 2010

7382042R0

Made in the USA
Lexington, KY
16 November 2010